Never Say Never

THE COMPLETE EXECUTIVE GUIDE
TO CRISIS MANAGEMENT

Len Biegel

Brick Tower Press
New York

Brick Tower Press
1230 Park Avenue
New York, New York 10128

© Len Biegel 2007

Library of Congress Cataloging-in-Publication Data
    Len Biegel
    Never Say Never, The Complete Executive Guide
                         to Crisis Management
    Includes index.
    ISBN 10: 1-883283-52-3
    ISBN 13: 978-1-883283-52-0
    1. Biegel, Len, —

    Business/Economics
    Insurance/Risk Assessment
    Nonfiction

    Library of Congress Control Number: 2007943580
    First Edition, January 2008

Contents

This book is dedicated to
Roberta, with deepest love

And to the memory of Uncle Sidney. This book would not
have been possible without his influence.

Acknowledgements

A book is born of influences, resources, and endless support. I am indebted to countless people at Royal Caribbean Cruises Ltd., and wish to express special thanks to Richard Fain, Chairman and CEO, who sets a high standard for what crisis preparedness and response should be; and to Adam Goldstein, President of Royal Caribbean International, who first suggested, "You know, this is a book you should write." To Carlos Campbell, who first introduced me to the National Association of Corporate Directors; to Peter Gleason, NACD's Chief Operating Officer for his insights; and to Suzanne Hopgood, co-author of *NACD's Board Leadership for the Company in Crisis*, for her perspective and updates on how forward-thinking board members are addressing the crisis preparedness issue.

Special thanks to my colleague Andy Gilman, for his countless thoughtful comments and his insights into what Jim Burke was like as a student of media training; and to Aydin Caginalp, formerly of Alston & Bird LLP, who kindly offered to introduce me to John Colby, publisher of Brick Tower Press; and to John Colby, for his commitment and support.

And most of all, with love and appreciation to my sons—Adam, for his support, guidance and inspiration, which are matched only by his molecular-level attention to detail, and Jonathan, who shows a keen understanding of how business should serve its customers; and to my wife Roberta, who is able to see around corners, and inspires and supports with unconditional love.

Introduction

Imagine that you are awakened from a deep sleep at 2:00 A.M. on Saturday. An automated emergency call system the company has recently subscribed to delivers the following message:

"This is the Action Plus Network with an urgent message. If this is Joe Doe, please enter your password, followed by the pound sign."

You comply with the instructions and hear the following:

"This is the Action Plus Network Emergency Line for ABC International. This call is to notify you that there is an emergency situation requiring your immediate presence at the Corporate Situation Room. If you are receiving this message and will be proceeding to the Situation Room, please press the star key, then hang up. If you need further assistance, please press nine."

You dress quickly and head for the office, which is about 20 minutes away. As you are driving, you switch on the radio and hear the news that explosions have hit eight international businesses, and two of those locations are owned by ABC International—in Kankakee Illinois, where 2,000 workers are employed in a round-the-clock chemical plant, and in London, where 200 sales and marketing staff are located.

By the time you reach the Situation Room, the lights are on and four other senior executives are there. As they scramble to decipher the controls on the new plasma TVs so they can find the news on CNN, word comes in that your CEO cannot be located. Someone thinks he's probably on the company plane headed back from a business meeting in Hong Kong. But no one is certain.

This is just the beginning of a crisis you thought you were prepared to face. But are you prepared?

Between 2000 and 2005—five short years—the unimagined happened. The United States was attacked on its own soil, sending New York City and the nation into shock; and then an entire city, New Orleans, was nearly destroyed in the worst natural disaster to hit the country.

As the 9/11 Commission concluded, "we must begin to imagine future disasters, perhaps multiple catastrophes, for they, too, may well occur." The most important failure, the report concluded, was one of imagination.

If 9/11 and Katrina have done nothing else, they should be a major wakeup call—an opportunity to prepare to survive.

Let's face it—there's a Tower of Babble out there ever since 9/11 and more recently Hurricane Katrina. It is all well-intentioned "do this, do that" information. But the simple amount of it is daunting, if not confusing. Add to that the years of accumulated advice from those in the trenches of management—especially Jack Welch and Andy Grove—some of whose sage advice is included in this book.

What needs sorting out is what's out there and what is most useful for you and your company. This all assumes you want to get better at crisis readiness. And then there's the group of companies out there that do little or nothing and intend to coast along. Well, that's where we get into the tough part: how to instill a crisis-readiness culture everywhere it belongs—and it does belong everywhere. It's not going to happen because more to-do lists pop up. It will happen because there are pressures, accountability and incentives—and we address that in this book as well.

The central themes of the book include the following:

The shocking events of 9/11 and Katrina showed, above all, the value of planning for crisis response and business continuity. And, from a CEO point of view, the urgent need to take charge of the process.

Are we as prepared as we should be? Not by a long shot! We're getting better. Will it take more wake-up calls? Or will it take commitment? It's up to you.

The executive traits required in a crisis are the same as the best traits required during non-crisis periods. The difference is that, in a crisis, you are working at warp speed and under enormous pressure.

Preparedness is a far better business choice than denial—and the second half of the book will detail the steps any company can and should take to be prepared.

But until there are generally accepted crisis preparedness, response and prevention standards in the US., and corporate boards assume official governance and hold senior management accountable, there is little or no likelihood that all American businesses will be as prepared as they should be.

Who is this book for?

This book is for every CEO, every board member, and every senior executive concerned about corporate reputation, in companies of all sizes—from the Fortune 500s to the small and medium-size companies—that do business with and are part of the private-sector supply chain that controls 85% of America's resources.

One may wonder why this book is aimed toward such a broad cross-section of American business. The answer is simple. We are all in the same boat, sharing a common set of threats and concerns in today's world. While every company has specific concerns, we have reached the point where we all have more in common than not—and that is what this book is based on.

There is a great deal of specific activity underway across industries—from banking to chemicals—working to help protect their physical assets. What this book is about is how to protect the other asset—reputation, and how, in a worst case situation, operations and market share must be protected with business continuity plans. Lose or weaken your reputation, and the consequences are as deep as and often deeper than any other loss. At the end of the day, it is about senior executive responsibility and accountability.

* * *

A Personal Note

In 1980, after several years in television (with CBS, Metromedia/Fox and public broadcasting), followed by consulting for the Israel Broadcasting Authority, the Shah of Iran, and the North Atlantic Treaty Organization (NATO), I joined public relations firm Burson-Marsteller. The initial assignment was to create a media department for the Washington office that would help clients understand the often adversarial relationship between business and the media.

In the midst of this assignment, in 1982, Johnson & Johnson, the maker of the popular pain-reliever Tylenol, received reports that several customers had died as the result of ingesting cyanide-laced Tylenol tablets.

As part of the small team assembled to help the client on the urgent and complex communications concerns, and having come from broadcasting where we survived by understanding the public, I thought the answers were obvious: Be quick to respond, show you care about the public, do something about the problem, and explain it all through regular contact with the media. And with something this serious, put the CEO forth as the spokesperson. Well, that is exactly what Jim Burke, the chairman of J&J, did. In doing so, he proved that the public will understand and forgive an honest, caring CEO (whose company, by the way, was a victim of the crime, not the cause) who was bold enough to recall the entire retail supply of Tylenol and commit to the design of a tamperproof pill and package. This swift, daring move worked. The brand eventually regained its market share, and the event marked the introduction of tamper-resistant packaging for almost all food and drug products.

Twenty-five years later, clients still remark that the counsel given to Jim Burke was brilliant. No, I am quick to reply, it was our collective good sense, given an understanding of the public and the media. It highlights, most of all, what a leader can accomplish when he asks for advice, considers it, combines it with his best instincts and moves quickly to protect his customers and products.

As with so many historic events—and this was without question an historic event—it takes time to realize its importance and to understand its long-term influence. As the dust began to settle—especially after it became clear that Tylenol in the tamperproof bottles was regaining its place among consumers—questions began surfacing about what this all meant. As the months unfolded, several of us in the media end of the PR business began realizing that perhaps a company could prepare. Perhaps we could develop some criteria and rules for management and communication during a crisis.

The result: The management of the Tylenol tamperings of 1982 was a landmark for modern day crisis management. It has become the textbook case for how to manage a crisis, and has spawned the modern day profession of crisis management.

Well, stay tuned as we unfold the highs (and a few lows) of crisis communications and management over the past 25 years, and as we consider what the Tylenol moment of 1982, a succession of other, earlier business crises, and the milestones of 9/11 and Hurricane Katrina mean for the CEO in today's vulnerable environment.

Much has happened on the political front over the past 25 years, with scandals, leadership ups and downs and the like. And while it is tempting to comment on those important areas, that would require an entirely separate volume, so I let them pass—with one exception. I have chosen to comment on the leadership under the incredible stress of 9/11—that is, the leadership of former NYC Mayor Rudy Giuliani.

Crisis preparedness is not simply about guarding the front door, building a war room, creating a business continuity plan, or conducting a fire drill. It's about all of it and more!

If timing is everything—or nearly everything—we likely are entering a new and potentially constructive era for the modern corporation. This new era, the Era of Accountability, is marked by a number of trends that remind the corporations that they are accountable to their owners, the shareholders—whether these shareholders are the moms and pops hoping to increase their assets or the giant investment funds trusted by their shareholders to protect and grow their assets. These assets, whether one share or a million, are entrusted to boards of directors. The best board members are objective, smart and experienced, and understand their fiduciary responsibilities to protect and grow the assets. The corporate scandals of the 1990s, highlighted by Tyco International, Enron and MCI, will have a lasting effect if they spur scrutiny of the stock exchanges, government and the shareholders to assure the most responsible board members.

An important new ingredient is growing on the governance to-do lists of many boards—and that is the protection of corporate reputation and assets through effective crisis prevention and readiness. If that trend continues, we are headed for the Never Say Never method of crisis management.

This shift toward accountability will not happen overnight. We have, in Part II, laid bare for the first time the steps needed to move from the gridlock in too many companies to Never Say Never readiness.

PART I

ARE WE READY?

1   Do We Have a Crisis or Don't We?

"When written in Chinese, the word crisis is composed of two characters. One represents danger, the other opportunity."
—John Fitzgerald Kennedy

Hold on! Do you even have a crisis? Not every event is a crisis. Regardless of the company, industry, location or size, every crisis, emergency and issue share common features. Let's get some definitions straight:

Crisis: A major event, generally characterized by one or more of the following:
- Possible or actual harm to individuals or property, including computer networks
- Imminent threat to "business as usual"
- Imminent threat to company or brand reputation
- National or international media attention—either immediate or potential

Emergency: A situation that is localized and controllable, such as a fire or injury. It generally is characterized by one or more of the following:
- Local media attention
- No substantial or uncontrollable threat to individuals or property
- Little or no disruption to operations
- No threat or indication of problems beyond the specific location.

Issue: A controversy, generally characterized by:
- Warnings through any number of sources—e.g., activist groups, legal claims, government investigations, research announcements, etc.
- Sufficient time to develop strategies and steps which may solve the problem before it escalates to a crisis
- No immediate harm or disruption to business.

AN ISSUE IS NOT A CRISIS.

Reactions to Crises

At the first signs of a crisis, reactions may be:
     Denial—"This can't be happening."
     Complacency—"If I ignore it, it may go away."
     Blame—"Who would dare do this?"

All of the above are dangerous and the wrong approach to take, though many companies do just that. The reality is that, as the old saying goes, "Where's there's smoke, there's fire." The sooner the fact-finding begins, the sooner the strategies for some solutions can take shape. This requires a mind-set that is willing to admit that something is wrong and that it is the company's responsibility to take charge—after all, if you don't, someone else will. And you will not like the results.

Successful crisis response requires:
–A plan
–Training and simulations
–Decisive leadership, combining rapid, thoughtful strategies and calm, well-tuned reactions—to get the facts, make decisions and act on them, and communicate to everyone concerned. But this takes some work.

While each event or crisis is different, or at least has different nuances and twists or turns, an effective crisis plan provides the framework for tackling any situation.

Soon after the Department of Homeland Security was formed, we began hearing a new phrase, "all hazards"—an important phrase to remind us that, though terrorism is the new big worry, we cannot and should not forget all the other hazards.

We live in a more complex world, which by definition carries more risks of possible disasters—from terrorism to widespread disease to natural disasters and hate crimes.

Are there tell-tale signs that a crisis is coming?

The answer is yes/maybe. Most crises take you by surprise. Others just might be on the horizon and can be spotted. It is worth considering some of the signs:
–Is there a nagging issue that simply will not go away?.
–Are there mounting complaints and agitation on customer or activist blogs?

—Has an investigative reporter called, alleging some irregularities?
—Is there a competitor in the midst of a crisis?
—Are employee suggestions being ignored?

An important note about terrorism

According to Rudy Giuliani, "part of the damage the terrorists hope to inflict is the emotional reaction in the wake of the destruction. The reason it's called 'terrorism' is that they want fear and its debilitating effects to linger long after the smoke has cleared. By preparing citizens for the possibility of a terrorist attack," Giuliani adds, "leaders can help minimize the emotional response in the wake of the destruction." (Rudolph W. Giuliani "Lessons of London: What's Next in War of Terror?" *USA Today*, July 11, 2005)

In 2005 the Homeland Security Council listed 15 nightmares. Take a look at the following scenarios:

Nuclear Detonation: 10-Kiloton Nuclear Device Terrorists drive a van with a nuclear device into the central business district of a major city and set it off.

Biological Attack: Aerosolized Anthrax Terrorists spray aerosolized anthrax from a van in three cities initially, followed by two more cities shortly afterward.

Biological Disease Outbreak: Flu Pandemic An influenza pandemic begins in south China and spreads within months to four major cities in the United States.

Biological Attack: Pneumonic Plague Terrorists release pneumonic plague into an airport bathroom, a sports arena and a train station in a major city, and it spreads rapidly.

Chemical Attack: Blister Agent Terrorists in a small aircraft spray a chemical blister agent over a packed college football stadium.

Chemical Attack: Toxic Industrial Chemicals Terrorists attack oil refineries with grenades and bombs; exploding cargo containers ignite ships, including one carrying toxic chemicals.

Chemical Attack: Nerve Agent Terrorists release sarin gas into the ventilation systems of three large office buildings in New York City.

Chemical Attack: Chlorine Tank Explosion Terrorists infiltrate an industrial storage facility and blow up a storage tank of chlorine, releasing a large quantity of the gas.

Natural Disaster: Major Earthquake A 7.2-magnitude earthquake occurs on a fault line through a major city, affecting six counties with a total population of 10 million.

Natural Disaster: Major Hurricane A category 5 hurricane with sustained winds of 160 miles per hour and storm surges of 20 feet hits a major metropolitan area.

Radiological Attack: "Dirty Bombs" Terrorists set off bombs with radioactive cesium-137 in three nearby moderate to large cities, contaminating 36 blocks in each.

Explosives Attack: Improvised Bombs Terrorists use handmade bombs, a large car or truck bomb and suicide belts to attack a sports stadium and an emergency room.

Biological Attack: Food Contamination Terrorists use liquid anthrax to contaminate batches of ground beef and orange juice that are distributed to different parts of the country.

Biological Attack: Foot-and-Mouth Disease Terrorists infect farm animals at several locations with foot-and-mouth disease, which spreads as the affected animals are transported.

Cyber Attack Over a period of several weeks, terrorists conduct cyber attacks on several parts of the nation's financial infrastructure.

(Source: Homeland Security Council,
reported in *The New York Times*, March 16, 2005)

This interesting and frightening list could go on for quite a stretch more., but it does illustrate the range of cataclysmic events we could face. In fact, Katrina was predicted rather accurately. If this list does not wake us to at least thinking about disaster and the consequences for business, what else will?

Are we prepared to face all these disasters? No. Would we collectively rise to the occasion? Yes, Americans have a collective sense of responsibilities in a disaster. We collect money; we donate food and clothing; companies sends goods and services; fire departments, rescue squads, hospitals all help each other. While there is ample evidence that more companies and organizations and local, state and federal agencies are better prepared since 9/11, we never can prepare for everything. But can we do a better job? Yes.

We can do a better job by:

- Closing the readiness gap, bringing the unprepared into the realm of the prepared.

- Creating a professional association concerned with setting standards, conducting training and sharing best practices in crisis preparedness.

- Holding CEOs and others accountable for preparedness.

More on this in Part II: Closing the Readiness Gap.

* * *

2   What We Know

In the post-9/11, post-Katrina world, we are faced with new regulatory threats, greater uncertainty, more complex risks, globalization and the 24/7 news cycle.

Crisis management as we know it today emerged after the Tylenol tamperings of the mid-1980s. While there are no "official" standards yet for effective crisis management, generally accepted standards have evolved over several years as a direct result of the public handling of the Tylenol case. Faced with sustained, unprecedented media coverage of this crime against an American icon, public affairs professionals began reflecting almost immediately on what this all meant: Could companies prepare for a crisis? Could they all do as well as Johnson & Johnson CEO Jim Burke did in handling a crisis? Could a crisis in fact be prevented?

In the twenty-five years since the Tylenol event, U.S. and global businesses have faced a host of crises of all dimensions. Some have been managed successfully—with success directly linked to the survival of corporate and brand reputation and/or market share. Others have failed spectacularly, with some of the worst involving the departure of the CEO. In a few remarkable cases we have actually seen the demise or severe restructuring of entire companies, such as Enron, Union Carbide and Tyco International, to name a few.

Is the glass three-quarters full or one-quarter empty?

In the latest Harris Interactive survey on crisis readiness in American business (December 2006), Harris first asked business leaders to tell them how much they worry about various crisis situations. Topping the list at 61%, not surprisingly, is compromise of corporate information systems. Terrorism came in next at 55%. And nearly half, or 45%, listed negative financial news. And, summing it all up, Harris found that 75% of businesses responding to the survey said they have a crisis plan. That also indicates that 25% do not have a crisis plan. Is this 25% in denial?

Eric Holdeman, director of emergency management for Seattle's King County, (an area prone to a significant earthquake threat) put it this way:

"There are four stages of denial. One is, it won't happen. Two is, if it does happen, it won't happen to me. Three: If it does happen, it won't be that bad. And four: If it happens to me and it's bad, there's nothing I can do to stop it anyway." (Source: Amanda Ripley, "Why We Don't Prepare for Disaster," *Time* August 20, 2006)

Jack and Suzy Welch offer some sage advice based on Jack's years of experience at GE:

"First, assume that the problem is worse than it appears. Skip the denial step, and get into the mind set that the problem will get bigger, messier, and more awful than you can possibly imagine.

"Second, assume there are no secrets in the world and that everyone will eventually find out everything.

"Third, assume you and your organization's handling of the crisis will be portrayed in the worst possible light. Define your own position early and often.

"Fourth, assume there will be changes in processes and people. Almost no crisis ends without blood on the floor.

"Fifth, assume your organization will survive, ultimately stronger for what happened."

—Jack Welch and Suzy Welch, *Winning* (HarperCollins, 2005)

Who have tested their plans?

According to a survey by Strohl Systems in the fall of 2006, 58% of U.S. organizations have exercised their business continuity plans in the past six months. 17% have never tested their plans, and nearly 7% tested their plan over a year ago. (Source: "Majority of U.S. Organizations Have Tested Business Continuity Plans in Last Six Months," *Continuity Central,* December 21, 2006)

Amid these indicators of business preparedness, or lack of it, some rather odd polling numbers have appeared that show that the general public thinks the nation is better prepared for events such as a pandemic or another terrorist attack than it really is. In survey results released by Columbia University in February, 2007, 46% of those surveyed said the nation has become better prepared in the last year. Dr. Irwin Redlener, director of the National Center for Disaster Preparedness at Columbia's Mailman school of Public Health, was stunned by the results. "There is no basis in reality for saying we're better off than we were a year ago, and nothing about our political, functional environment should give anybody any confidence that it's improved." (Source: Richard Perez-Pena, "A Perception of Progress on Disaster Preparedness," *New York Times*, February 20, 2007)

What you need to do

Crisis management professionals know that companies who do better in a crisis are those that:

–Embrace an all-hazards approach to crisis planning. While 9/11 and Katrina stand out, we face dozens of other types of crises An effective plan can equip a company to handle any event because a structure, with well-trained and practiced procedures, is in place.

–Understand that the war on terrorism is a long-term battle and may directly or indirectly affect any company at any time. Francis Frago Townsend, Assistant to the President for Security and Counterterrorism put it this way: "When you talk about the threat, you have to talk about the enemy. The enemy is fractured, it is degraded, but it's not less lethal. I think it's important that people understand that. We worry about the aviation threat. When you look at things like the London plot—you know, it's funny, it's been termed the 'London plot,' but that's clearly a misnomer because, while the launching point for it was London, it was a plot directed at the United States, at killing U.S. citizens and causing U.S. economic damage and fracturing the relationship of a critical ally in Great Britain. So we know that if anyone needed proof of the continued threat, August [2006] should have been it." (Source: David W. Silverberg, "Assessing the Threat," *HS Today,* January, 2007)

–Understand that effective crisis management requires leadership—and this includes your commitment to direct responsibility for both crisis readiness and response should a crisis occur. This means that readiness is not a sometime, expendable activity. In the most effective companies, it is a required responsibility. While many companies have effective crisis plans in place, there is also ample evidence to suggest that for many it remains a sometime activity, simulations and training are easily postponed, or the crisis preparation function is not coordinated at a senior level.

–Show they care about their employees, customers, shareholders and the public.

–Openly and quickly share the facts—good and bad—with their customers and the public.

–Accept blame when they are at fault.

–Continuously examine their vulnerabilities.

–Prepare and practice.

–Learn from mistakes—theirs and others'.

But ... to what degree are the CEO and other senior execs involved? I was asked not long ago by the CEO of a Fortune 50 company to tell him what I thought he ought to do to assure that his company is crisis-ready.

The answer:
Assume personal responsibility for making sure that the company is crisis-ready. Make certain that all plans are as short as possible. (In fact, the best plan should fit in your shirt pocket.) Make a commitment to practice, practice, practice, practice!

While some CEOs have assumed more direct responsibility for crisis preparedness and response, some companies or industries persist in sheltering the CEO from the realities of what could be massive threats to the organization. In the airline industry, for example, the tradition had generally called for the CEO to avoid any public appearances—especially before the media—when a crash occurred, until many hours had passed and there was some evidence of the cause. This began to change in response to the events of 9/11. In another example, this involving a drug company, the rule at one time was to avoid letting the CEO know of any product-related deaths until a magic number of 6 or more had been reached.

Share price is a big concern—even bigger when a crisis strikes. According to a report by the Corporate Executive Board, "The willingness of the financial community to punish missteps is attention-getting, but would not raise a serious alarm if the stock price damage were temporary." The study found that 41% of the companies that experienced a shock (i.e., a 30% decline) to their share price took a year to recover. But 32% never recovered. ("Refocusing Reputation Management," The Corporate Executive Board, 2004)

Reputation matters, especially in the eyes of Wall Street. A clear majority—88%—of analysts say reputation is important. It is scored even a shade higher in Europe, with 91% emphasizing the importance, and yet higher—94%— by analysts in Asia and the Pacific. (Source: Hill & Knowlton *Corporate Reputation Watch*, May 31, 2006)

An ounce of prevention pays big dividends when a crisis hits.

The speed at which change can occur today, and the impact it can have, increase the need for crisis planning. "The speed and broader impact of change increases business risk and reduces viable reaction time. This makes preparing for change and crisis more critical than ever—especially since corporations are often judged more harshly for their responses to a crisis rather than the fact that they had a crisis in the first place." (Report of the NACD Blue Ribbon Commission on Risk Oversight, 2002, 2003, 2006)

Special interest and activist organizations know how to attract attention. Even the threat to harm a brand's market share through boycotts and other exploits will often call a company to action. While most boycotts have only succeeded in causing considerable angst for companies, there are a few that do stand out for having achieved their goals. For example, pressure on McDonald's by the National Heart Savers Association forced reduction in the use of fats in some of their fried foods, and led to changes in menu options. Animal activists nearly destroyed the fur coat industry through boycotts and public demonstrations. Ongoing opposition to bioengineered foods in Europe and the U.S. have limited the growth of this emerging technology. And, most recently, shareholder activists played a big role in the ouster of Bob Nardelli as CEO of The Home Depot.

The blogs are here, with enormous potential to help spot problems early on. Just think of the power of consumers or activists to create blogs telling of problems or perceived injustices and, in worst case situations, to spread rumors and threats.

How well prepared are we? Or are we not?

The bigger the company, the better the readiness picture. Ninety-seven percent of the Fortune 200 companies have an emergency response plan that has been updated since the 9/11 terrorist attacks. Nearly 90% of the companies test their emergency plans each year, and 40% test their plans at least twice each year.

More than half of the companies (54%) said that security-related issues are part of the board's regular corporate governance activities, and 81% of companies that raised security to a board-level issue did so in the two years after 9/11. (Source: The Business Roundtable, March 2004)

According to a September 2006 Harris Interactive survey of US-based senior executives, 46% indicate their companies are more prepared compared to the prior year in their ability to access data in a catastrophe. Yet 39% give their companies grades of C or lower—citing inconsistent practices, lack of preparedness and competing priorities. Specifically, email and telecommunications appear to be the most vulnerable in a cyber attack, power failure or other disaster. Spending? Fifty-eight percent of the respondents report no increase in spending to reduce the risk of loss of business data. (Source: "US Companies Better Prepared to Protect Business-Critical Information and Data Than a Year Ago," *Continuity Central*, September 5, 2006)

The area most improved since 9/11 is technology. While not perfect, it is far better than before. The financial industry has made heavy investments in redundancy and protective measures to keep our banks and stock exchanges running in the event of an attack. This is encouraging, in light of the essential role technology plays in our economy, and as an antidote to the oft-mentioned motives of the terrorist who sees our economy as a prime target. On other levels, such as physical security and access to buildings and plants, there is a checkerboard of systems, from some highly secure buildings in New York City to the virtual fortress surrounding Washington's House and Senate offices to virtually nothing in office buildings in some cities.

Succession planning presents another big void. If the CEO suddenly cannot function, for reasons of health or other absence, someone needs to take over immediately. According to a survey by Korn/Ferry International, more than 60% of companies worldwide do not have a capable CEO-in-waiting. (Source: "Most Major Corporations Unprepared for Potential Succession Needs, According to Global Survey Of Recruiters," press release, Korn/Ferry International, May 3, 2005

Globalization has created vast new markets, and outsourcing key functions such as call centers and data processing has become the norm. But challenges abound that, if left unchecked, could open the door to crises. Consider, for example, that only half the offshore organizations use passwords for entry to data systems they are managing (in contrast, 78% of U.S.

organizations have strict password rules), and 50% admit that more than half their users are not in compliance with their information security policies.

The result: Extortion, fraud and intellectual property theft occurred in 2005 at one in every five or six Indian companies—rates that are double and even quadruple the rest of the world. Reports are that India is catching up–but in the meantime, the concerns remain. (Source: "The Global State of Information Security 2006," *Continuity Central*, September 25, 2006.)

The news media thrive on chaos. And news travels at the speed of light. Technology is changing the rules of journalism, enabling anyone to report news on the Web or send reports, photos and videos to traditional news outlets. This all doubtless will have some affect on journalism— though time will tell how and to what extent, as the public makes choices on how they perceive all this information.

Prevention is possible if you have tight controls and ethics standards, and review them regularly and enforce them. Training plays a big role in all of this—so that everyone, without exception, knows the rules of the road. Listen to employees for prevention ideas—in the old suggestion box or in its new electronic forms. Look at drills as a template for identifying areas that can be changed or improved, preventing a crisis.

When a crisis hits, stand up and be counted—in the first minutes if possible. If not, others will start speaking up and interpreting, speculating and guessing. And you may never catch up. Look, for example, at the stable of "experts" CNN and the other news outlets have on tap to comment in crises. They may be experienced people, but they generally have no knowledge at all about your crisis. They are simply speculators.

Open communication leads to trust, and trust is what you need in a crisis—from employees, customers, shareholders and lawmakers. As Harold Burson, founder of Burson-Marsteller, puts it, "By taking the offensive and addressing the concerns, real and imagined, of key audiences, a company is more likely to be viewed as a responsible and responsive citizen rather than a recalcitrant or indifferent monolith." ("Crisis Management," undated white paper)

And finally—we are not alone. Until 9/11, American companies had not experienced an act of terror on U.S. soil. Nations around the world have become increasingly concerned since 9/11. England has had their share of terror scares and attacks, but no other nation has been struck by more bombings and continued to function at top speed than Israel.

My family and I lived in Israel for six months several years ago. What was striking was the way security was and still is a part of life. Briefcases and purses were searched when entering a bank, a large shop, a movie theater, a museum. Soldiers were everywhere, carrying submachine guns on the streets. Radios played in the buses, delivering the latest news for all. But life went on; security is a way of life.

Eyal Kaplan. General Partner, Walden Israel Venture Capital, summed up crisis readiness among Israeli businesses: "[M]aybe military training makes us defiant. We have to prove to the world that they made a mistake when they didn't invest in Israel because of the terrorist situation. And every businessperson I know feels the same way. We are driven to show the world how good we are, especially during times of crises."

"Here, we are all in this together," he continued. "In Israel, we are a group-oriented culture. Always be a David in attitude, even though you may be a Goliath in assets."

Israel has been guarding the country's assets so long their security is often looked at as a model. Danny Halpern, a financial consultant in Israel, put it this way: "If we have one guard in front of a mall that has been bombed, America will put up ten guards before the people are reassured. Here, I believe we invest more in the quality of our security people and less in the mechanics. In America, because of the huge numbers, the investment is in the mechanics—the system—and then they hire minimum-wage security staff. Here it's the opposite." (Source: Dan Carrison, *Business Under Fire* (Amacom, 2004))

* * *

3   The Wakeup Calls—Lessons Learned, Lessons Ignored

Sept. 11 and Katrina brought calls to build impregnable walls against such tragedies ever occurring again. But despite the vows, both New Orleans and the nation's security apparatus remain dangerously leaky. 'People call these crises wakeup calls,' says Dr. Irwin Redlener, associate dean of Public Health at Columbia University and director of the National Center for Disaster Preparedness. 'But they're more like snooze alarms. We get agitated for a while, and then we don't follow through.'" (Jeffrey Kluger, "Why We Worry About the Things We Shouldn't," *Time*, December 4, 2006)

The crises described in the following pages are a cross-section of high profile crises and a few lesser known. They have been chosen to illustrate important lessons learned, but are not intended as an encyclopedia of crises.

A Quick Walk Back in Time

The Triangle Shirtwaist Fire

On a Saturday afternoon in 1911, the Triangle Shirtwaist Company factory on the eighth, ninth and tenth floors of a "fireproof" building off Washington Square in New York City became the scene of a massive tragedy in which 141 young men and women factory workers perished, unable to escape the flames and smoke from a fire which erupted among highly flammable fabrics. Many escaped down the stairs before the fire spread; others were cut off by flames and, seeing no other way out, jumped to their deaths. No one except the factory's owners, who escaped, knew of the way to safety through the roof

The Triangle Shirtwaist fire illustrated a fact well known to NYC garment workers at that time—that most garment factories were potential firetraps, with bins of highly flammable textiles and patterns surrounded by smoking workers and overworked sewing machines that sometimes overheated and caused small fires. In fact, the Triangle Shirtwaist Company had already been cited for fire safety concerns.

After

The incident led to a number of reforms—but not before the insensitive local Manufacturers' Association called a meeting to find ways to avoid the reforms to protect workers.

The Triangle Shirtwaist fire of 1911 would change the way government regulates worker safety. Before the fire, government had mostly stayed away from businesses, feeling it had no authority to regulate them. The Triangle Shirtwaist fire remains as a turning point in U.S. history. Countless state and federal laws were enacted because of this incident, and unions gained numerous new workers who wanted someone to fight for their safety.

In a more perfect world, with more fire safety regulations, more people would have escaped from the World Trade Center on 9/11, 90 years later.

The Sinking of the Titanic

The RMS *Titanic*, considered unsinkable, sailed under international laws governing the number of lifeboats on a ship which were, to say the least, loose. In 1912, the *Titanic* sailed with only 20 lifeboats capable of carrying 1,178 people for the 2,223 passengers and 899 crew on board. Had there been enough seats for everyone, many more would have survived. In the years that followed, international regulations were strengthened considerably, and today's passenger and cruise ships follow very strict guidelines for adequate lifeboat capacity for passengers and crew.

The lifeboat issue aside, the calamity could have been avoided altogether. The captain had received several radio warnings from other ships to watch for ice in the North Atlantic, and the crow's nest did watch for the ice, though the seamen on the lookout did not have binoculars (a curious lapse that has never been explained.) By the time the huge, black ice formation was spotted, and despite quick attempts to reverse the ship's engines, it was simply too late.

In 1912, long before today's mass media coverage of Senate hearings, the *Titanic* hearing was a major occasion, lasting 17 days.

Senator William Alden Smith: Suppose you had glasses [binoculars] ... could you have seen this black object [the iceberg] at a greater distance?

Lookout Frederick Fleet: We could have seen it a bit sooner.

Smith: How much sooner?

Fleet: Well, enough to get out of the way.

J. Bruce Ismay, president of the White Star Line, the British owner of the *Titanic*, also testified, speaking here about his experience after jumping into a lifeboat fairly early in the crisis:

Smith: You did not see her go down?

Ismay: No, sir.

Smith: How far were you from the ship?

Ismay: I do not know how far we were away. I was sitting with my back to the ship. I was rowing all the time I was in the boat. We were pulling away.

Smith: You did not see her go down?

Ismay: I am glad I did not.

("Word for Word: The *Titanic Disaster*, *New York Times*, Dec. 28, 1997)

After

Additional boats were immediately installed on North Atlantic ships. And within a year, international regulations required muster drills and lifeboats for everyone.

Modern Times

Terrorists Hijack the S.S. *Achille Lauro*

In October 1985, four members of the Palestine Liberation Front held the passengers of the cruise chip *Achille Lauro* hostage off the Egyptian coast, demanding that Israel release 50 Palestinian prisoners. Wielding weapons they had brought on board, they shot wheelchair-bound American passenger Leon Klinghoffer and threw his body overboard. The hijackers, boarding the ship with the other passengers, had slipped on board without so much as an inspection, which might have revealed their weapons.

After

Like the sinking of the *Titanic*, this incident led to maritime reforms—this time an overhaul of security practices aboard passenger vessels.

Challenges on Today's Oceans The rapidly growing cruise industry had immediate reasons to tighten security after 9/11, given the concerns of the traveling public. With bigger ships on order, some carrying more than 4,000 guests and 1,000-plus crewmembers, everyone needed assurances. Royal Caribbean Cruises' leadership, along with others in the industry, moved faster than any other business in the United States to tighten access to the ships with photos embedded in what is known as the SeaPass Card. Security staffing was increased, and every item coming on board at any time—whether luggage or supplies—is subjected to x-ray screening or other means, including highly trained canines.

Cargo ship screening—admittedly a more complex challenge—continues to be debated among shippers and port security officials. Some form of technology will doubtless be the answer, but decisions could be a long way off.

And finally, port security, specifically for authorization of people entering for business reasons, continues to be inconsistent, with a checkerboard of procedures. The guards at the gates at many ports continue to be among the lowest-level security available, and some often do not even know who they work for.

Tylenol: The Big Wakeup Call

The 1982 Tylenol tampering crisis marked the birth of modern-day crisis management. Johnson & Johnson's handling of the crime against innocent consumers and against the Tylenol brand established solid criteria:
−Be quick to respond.
−Show you care about the public.
−Do something about the problem.
−Explain it all through regular contact with the media.

Throughout the crisis, J&J's CEO, Jim Burke, showed how to be direct and caring, and that a corporation can show a strong and compassionate face.

The Tylenol Tampering and the Birth of 20th Century Crisis Management

"Cases of full disclosure in business abound, but Johnson & Johnson probably set the gold standard with its handling of the Tylenol crisis in the 1980s."

—Jack Welch and Suzy Welch, *Winning*

In 1982, seven people in the Chicago area died after taking Tylenol (a product of Johnson's McNeil Pharmaceutical division) that had been laced with cyanide. Until then, product tampering was a rare event in a world of easy-to-open bottles and packages. These poisonings remain an unsolved mystery.

Johnson & Johnson's handling of the Tylenol tampering may be remembered most for J&J chairman Jim Burke's quick decision to protect the public by recalling the entire supply of Tylenol from the nation's retail shelves; communicating openly with the public; and, in less than three months, introducing a newly formed product in tamperproof packaging. By any stretch, this was a difficult decision, given the product's 35% share of the $1 billion analgesic market—and the fact that Tylenol contributed about 20% of J&J's profits.

In the midst of the crisis, J&J commissioned substantial opinion polling and found that 87% of the public realized J&J was not responsible for the murders, though 61% said they were not likely to buy extra-strength capsules again. Tylenol did rebound. And company morale soared.

On February 10, 1986, history repeated itself when J&J and the Food and Drug Administration again received a report of a death linked to the lacing of Tylenol capsules with cyanide.

The management of the landmark Tylenol tampering crisis was not merely about a compassionate and effective communication program. The re-introduction of Tylenol in tamper-proof packaging heralded the beginning of tamperproof packaging for nearly every food, drug and small consumer package found on store shelves today.

Robert Kniffen, J&J's vice president of corporate relations at the time, commented on the decision process and the J&J Credo:

"I was in the president's office at McNeil Consumer and he had asked the vice president of finance to compute what it would cost to recall

all of the capsules in the United States. This guy came back and said he calculated that it would be seventy-five million dollars. And then he said, 'but we don't have seventy-five million dollars.' Then there was a pause and another guy said, 'But how can we not do this, because there might be another bottle on the shelf, and if we don't get them back, someone might die.' It was not an instance when someone said, 'Let's consult the Credo and think through this problem, starting with our responsibility to the consumer,' but rather it was away of looking at the world, at business, and at the decisions. The Credo structures the way you think about things. When all that was done and the dust had settled, we reached the conclusion that those hundreds of individual decisions were right decisions. They sprang from some common way of looking at the world, which in retrospect was the Credo."

"I was convinced we were going to lose the brand," continued Kniffen. "As the result of that (the recall), we did find three bottles on the shelves in Chicago that were poisoned."

—Patricia Jones and Larry Kahaner,
Say It and Live It (Doubleday, 1985)

Burke commented at the time: "After the crisis was over, we realized that no meeting had been called to make the first critical decision. Every one of us knew what we had to do. We had the Credo to guide us." Kniffen explains, "At Johnson & Johnson there is no mission statement that hangs on the wall. Instead, for more than 60 years, a simple, one-page document—our Credo—has guided our actions in fulfilling our responsibilities to our customers, our employees, the community and our stockholders. Our worldwide Family of Companies shares this value system in 36 languages spreading across Africa, Asia/Pacific, Eastern Europe, Europe, Latin America, Middle East and North America." (Source: Patricia Jones and Larry Kahaner, *Say It and Live It*)

Our Credo

We believe our first responsibility is to the doctors, nurses and patients,
    to mothers and fathers and all others who use our products and services.
In meeting their needs everything we do must be of high quality.
We must constantly strive to reduce our costs in order to maintain reasonable prices.
Customers' orders must be serviced promptly and accurately.
Our suppliers and distributors must have an opportunity to make a fair
    profit.

We are responsible to our employees, the men and women who work
with us throughout the world.
Everyone must be considered as an individual.

We must respect their dignity and recognize their merit.
They must have a sense of security in their jobs.
Compensation must be fair and adequate, and working conditions clean,
orderly and safe.
We must be mindful of ways to help our employees fulfill their family
responsibilities.
Employees must feel free to make suggestions and complaints.
There must be equal opportunity for employment, development and
advancement for those qualified.
We must provide competent management, and their actions must be just
and ethical.

We are responsible to the communities in which we live and work and to
the world community as well.
We must be good citizens—support good works and charities and bear
our fair share of taxes.
We must encourage civic improvements and better health and education.
We must maintain in good order the property we are privileged to use,
protecting the environment and natural resources.

Our final responsibility is to our stockholders.
Business must make a sound profit.
We must experiment with new ideas.
Research must be carried on, innovative programs developed and mis-
takes paid for.
New equipment must be purchased, new facilities provided and new
products launched.
Reserves must be created to provide for adverse times.
When we operate according to these principles, the stockholders should
realize a fair return.

Jim Collins, author of *Good to Great*, talks about an event that
occurred three years before the Tylenol tampering, when Burke "pulled 20
key executives into a room and thumped his finger on a copy of the J&J
Credo. Penned 36 years earlier by R.W. Johnson Jr., it laid out the 'We hold
these truths to be self-evident' of the Johnson & Johnson Co., among them
a higher duty to 'mothers and all others that use our products.' Burke wor-
ried that executives had come to view the Credo as an artifact … . 'I said,

"Here's the Credo. If we're not going to live by it, let's tear it off the wall."' Burke later told Joseph Badaracco and Richard Ellsworth for their book, *Leadership and The Quest for Integrity,* '[T]he room erupted into a debate that ended with recommitment. Burke and his colleagues would conduct similar meetings around the world, reviving the Credo as a living document.'" (Jim Collins, "What These Extraordinary Leaders Can Teach Today's Troubled Executives," *Fortune*, July 21, 2003)

At the November, 1982, press conference reintroducing Tylenol, Jim Burke said:

"It is our job at Johnson & Johnson to ensure the survival of Tylenol, and we are pledged to do this. While we consider this crime an assault on society, we are nevertheless ready to fulfill our responsibility, which includes paying the price of this heinous crime. But I urge you not to make Tylenol the scapegoat.

"I am confident that the news media, working in its own way and according to its own dictates, will help us to dispel these fears about a product that rightfully earned the confidence of the public. We welcome any help we can get from you and others in the vast rebuilding task that lies ahead."

After

The Food and Drug Administration enacted regulations requiring that over-the-counter drugs and certain medical devices and cosmetic products be marketed in tamper-resistant packages. Second, Congress enacted the Federal Anti-Tampering Act, which gives authority to the FDA, U.S. Department of Agriculture and the FBI to follow up on tampering violations, requiring penalties, including fines and imprisonment, for tampering or falsely reporting tampering.

I am often asked about what all of this meant and how it came to spawn an entire public affairs specialty. While the advice to be open, candid, decisive, and responsive to the public was sound, the real credit for the successful handling of the crisis goes to Jim Burke. The solid advice he received validated not only his best instincts but the strength of the company's corporate Credo. Through the simplicity of his messages, empathy for every customer and the decisive action to recall the product, Burke was able to transcend the stereotype of the monolithic, anonymous corporation, and limit the damage to the brand.

Andy Gilman, CEO of CommCore Consulting Group, coached Jim Burke for his countless media appearances during the crisis. He shared some of his thoughts:

"My initial impressions were that he was a no-nonsense CEO. But he was also one of the few CEOs I met who was passionately concerned with the customers. Many have learned how to say the appropriate words of concern; I got the sense that Burke was serious about this. I recall one prep session for the national satellite press conference to announce the return of Tylenol to the shelves. Burke gave an answer to a question according to the prepared Q&A. It was adequate, but he didn't feel the answer was good enough for the public. He said, 'I need more information that will help customers before I answer that.' The question that John Stossel asked him during one of the "20/20" interviews typified Burke's attitude. Stossel played a tape in which Burke choked up as he announced the death of one of the victims of the poisonings. Burke then went on to talk about some business and customer plans. The quote I believe from Stossel was that 'you mix decency with cunning...'" (Source: Interview by author)

J&J's famous Credo meant something. There was a values system in place. They also had deposits of goodwill in their PR bank.

They did make smart decisions. They pulled a strong team together and worked on it. They went above and beyond what they had to do. The government at first did not require tamper proof packaging, and certainly not triplicate seals.

The Credo was not discussed in every meeting, but its philosophy permeated their thinking. It's similar to a code of ethics; once it's been taught to a group, family or society, they make decisions with this embedded in their thought process. One of the morals: "Is this the right thing to do?"

The FDA has noticed that when one tampering occurs, a number of other incidents generally occur in rapid succession. In the months and years that followed, the FDA was involved in a widespread series of investigations that included dozens of products, most notably Gerber baby food, Girl Scout cookies, and more over-the-counter drugs. This suggests a pattern of "copy-cat" tamperings, which could be attributed to a desire by some consumers for either attention or the quick settlement of fraudulent monetary claims. Whether these are false alarms or petty legal claims, they occasionally create increasing pressures on companies.

To Recall or Not to Recall?

Pepsi and the Needle Hoax

Several years after the Tylenol episodes, a Tacoma, Washington, man claimed he had found a syringe in a can of Diet Pepsi. A media frenzy began as several similar claims were made. Pepsi management and the FDA, perplexed by the claims, conducted thorough searches and investigations, which showed that such claims were impossible. Pepsi even proved it by showing the details of the canning process on TV news programs across the nation.

As Dr. David Kessler, FDA Commissioner said at the time, "You never say never, and certainly we are inspecting. But tampering would certainly be difficult to do." (Source: Martin Tolchin, "U.S. Official Has Doubts About Pepsi Tampering." *The New York Times*, June 17, 1993)

After nearly a week of headlines and more copycat claims, an in-store surveillance camera showed a customer boldly slipping a syringe into a Diet Pepsi can. FDA Commissioner Kessler then officially ended the crisis by declaring it was a hoax.

Pepsi's frequent and clear communications to the public were reminiscent of the Tylenol crisis—and, interestingly, were driven in large measure by Pepsi's corporate credo, which states that customer safety comes first and that communication should be fast and open.

Throughout the week, Pepsi stood firm in its decision not to issue a recall order—believing that to have done so would have given the criminals more satisfaction. Had there been any deaths, the recall decision would likely have been different. The stock price held firm throughout the week.

Each day, from the start, Pepsi conducted a daily survey of 150 consumers. When asked to react to the statement, "I feel the Pepsi-Cola Company is handling the issue in a responsible manner, the days averaged an 85% affirmation. (Source "The Pepsi Hoax: What Went Wrong," The Pepsi-Cola Company, 1993)

Looking at the consumers-turned-criminals behind this crisis, Stanton Samenow, author of *Inside the Criminal Mind*, referred to those who tamper with cans or make copycat claims. "It's absolute personal glorification and satisfaction when he or she sits back and watches an entire nation react just baffled. It's a feeling of power and control, he has outsmarted the nation. Everyone is talking about it." (Source: "For Copycats, 'A Feeling of Power, Control,'" *USA Today*, June 17, 1993,

Glass in Gerber Baby Food

Following a report that a mother in New York had found pieces of glass in a jar of Gerber baby food, Gerber was faced with the tough decisions all consumer product companies face when they get news of this sort. Do we recall the product? And if not, what do we do?

Gerber, like Pepsi, stood fast and did not issue a recall, but did an exhaustive investigation of the batch in question and found no glass. Copycat reports flowed in, and Gerber checked on every one. Nonetheless, public confidence and market share dropped, but were restored to nearly their original levels after a vigorous public relations and marketing program—which included tours of the plants for reporters, a mailing to 2.6 households showing the proper way to open a jar, and an ongoing communication program to employees, doctors, trade customers and government authorities.

Benzene in Perrier

Perrier, long considered the icon of bottled water, shocked the U.S. public in 1990 when North Carolina health officials discovered low levels of benzene in the water. Benzene is a carcinogen. The company first responded that this was an isolated incident caused by an operator error at one plant. When it soon was learned that the benzene was in the product in Europe as well, an angry public forced a worldwide recall of Perrier—an immediate blow to their market share as other bottled waters took their place in bars and on grocery shelves.

Coca-Cola

Another beverage icon, Coca-Cola, withdrew 15 million cans of various soft drinks in Belgium when consumers reported a number of problems, including the hospitalization of 40 students with symptoms of food poisoning.

In 1999, Coke took a beating in Europe after a series of events overwhelmed the company—including the carbon dioxide in the soda being tainted with sulfur, and a fungicide attaching itself to the bottoms of cans. The European offices did not notify Atlanta HQ of the problems until three days after the emergencies. Had they notified Atlanta immediately, as good practice dictates, Atlanta might have asked the right questions and supported the Europe operations—avoiding denials which led to headlines and loss of faith in Coke.

By 2002, product recalls for a variety reasons—from defects to tamperings—had risen so much that the public was ignoring a good many of them.

Recalls—Lessons Learned

When the dust from the Tylenol tamperings had settled, public affairs professionals and many companies renewed their efforts to understand how crises arise and how responses should be fashioned. What we concluded was that crisis management follows a pattern:

The pre-crisis stage: Companies begin to identify potential risks or problems, develop crisis plans, and conduct simulations and training to prepare employees to handle crises, and take steps to prevent some crises from even happening.

The crisis stage (if one occurs): Companies, guided by their crisis plans, assess the situation, begin to investigate the cause(s) of the crisis, take actions to end it, and communicate this information to a host of stakeholders. The role of the CEO is especially important in this stage, and the Tylenol legacy has a lasting effect by identifying Jim Burke as the role model for the spokesperson under fire—calm, compassionate, decisive, and out front.

The post-crisis or recovery stage: If the crisis significantly impacts the business, continue operations in some altered way and repair possible damage to brand reputation, share price and corporate reputation.

The BIG Wakeup Calls: 9/11 and Katrina

"Nothing surprises me after September 11, 2001. I think I took that word out of my vocabulary after that incident."

—Rudy Giuliani

September 11, 2001, was one of those crystal clear sunny days, a seemingly perfect day on the East Coast. Washington, D.C., traffic was heavy that day; I arrived at the office a bit later then usual and was welcomed by about a half dozen staff members standing in front of the TV set in front of my desk. They were gazing in horror at the scene on CNN showing the World Trade Center with smoke pouring from one of the towers. Neither they nor CNN knew what really had happened. The phone rang a moment later, with a call from client American Airlines. "We don't know what's going on, but we're going to need help. Could you get staff to Dulles, JFK and LAX to stand by in case they're needed?"

The wheels were set in motion immediately, and we worked through the next hours and days helping American Airlines with logistics and communications. There was no turning back. This was a moment that would change America.

"We are entering a period in which a small number of people, operating without overt state sponsorship but using the enormous power of modern computers, biogenetic pathogens, air transport and even smaller nuclear weapons, will be able to exploit the tremendous vulnerabilities of modern societies." (Philip Bobbitt, "Get Ready for the Next Long War," *Time*, September 9, 2002)

On 9/11, lack of information about evacuation routes and procedures became a major hindrance to those who did try to escape. Though much had been done to assure safe building evacuations and fire safety in the wake of the Triangle Shirtwaist fire, it is shocking to realize that only 45% of 445 World Trade Center survivors had known the building had three stairwells. And only half knew the doors to the roof were locked.

The unprecedented events of 9/11, of far greater proportion than any disaster in United States history, provided another wakeup call, showing that the unthinkable may occur. Katrina, by contrast, was predictable. It was only a matter of time until a category 5 hurricane struck the New Orleans and the Gulf region.

Then Hurricane Katrina, the nation's worst natural disaster, hit the Gulf region in 2005. It's been said that it was a miracle that so many companies have been able to function in the region. It's no miracle. Those that quickly resumed operations had plans.

While it is widely acknowledged that the federal government failed after Hurricane Katrina, many companies were able to activate their disaster plans and do a heroic job despite lack of electrical power and security. The biggest challenge, amid this backdrop of chaos, was how to help their employees put their lives back together. The plans that worked best—and these include those of The Home Depot, Wal-Mart, BellSouth, Folgers, Oreck and others—were detailed in every aspect. What made them work, too, is these companies' low tolerance for red tape, can-do attitudes and strong support from their main offices.

One of the basic concerns in the wake of a hurricane is the massive structural damage to homes and businesses. While most states have strict building codes to protect against disasters, not all do. After Katrina,

Louisiana looked at mandatory building codes, joining another hurricane-prone state, Florida. Florida's code, on the books since 2001, is generally believed to protect structures in winds as high as 120 mph. Mississippi, also hit by Katrina, still has no statewide code.

On the whole, big businesses fared better than the small ones, but few have come away without deep scars. Hotels, restaurants and casinos, once the lifeblood of the city, have been slow to recover.

A *Time* magazine poll one year later (August 20, 2006) found that only 16% of New Orleans' citizens said they were "very well prepared" for the next one. (Source: Amanda Ripley, "Why We Don't Prepare for Disaster," *Time* August 20, 2006)

An inside look at FedEx's disaster preparedness system presents an interesting picture.

"Emergency central is a big, dimly lit room on the fourth floor of its new Global Operations Control in Memphis. John Dunavant is the GOC's chief; it's his job to make sure the hundreds of planes and thousands of trucks arrive when they're supposed to, and to have a sure-fire backup plan when they don't. A large screen at the front of the room shows the position, origin, and destination of every aircraft FedEx currently has in the sky ... . [With] such events as an air-traffic-controller strike in France and blackout in Los Angeles ... it's no wonder that FedEx gets so much practice in flexibility. What's more, FedEx conducts disaster drills several times a year—for everything from big earthquakes to bioterrorism to a monster typhoon hitting the company's hub in the Philippines. Eight disaster kits, each containing two tons of such supplies as fuel and communications gear, stand ready in Memphis in case a facility is in need of repair." (Ellen Florian Kratz, "For FedEx it Was Time to Deliver," *Fortune*, October 3, 2005)

The FedEx GOC became a major resource during Katrina—delivering ice, home generators and water to Baton Rouge and Tallahassee, providing an enormous survival link for FedEx employees. And, like others, FedEx delivered countless shipments of emergency supplies for the Red Cross.

What did FedEx learn from all this?

As FedEx told CNN:

–Lesson #1: Arrange for temporary housing in advance for employees who might get displaced.

–Lesson #2: Don't count on cell phones. The local networks were down for days after the storm; the company is increasing the number of satellite phones it deploys. (Source: CNN broadcast, October, 2007

One of the biggest lessons learned for all was that security is a big issue in a disaster like Katrina. In the desperate days following the storm, looting was a big issue. When the railroads, for example, placed portable generators at switching points, they were stolen within moments.

The much smaller Oreck, the maker of vacuum cleaners with a plant in the region, also had a plan and a strategy.

"If they were an Oreck employee before the hurricane, they still have a job," was the loud and clear declaration of Tom Oreck, the company's president and CEO. Against all odds, the company brought temporary housing, generators, food, water and supplies to their employees in the region. By September 9, less than 2 weeks after the hurricane struck, the Gulfport plant, with 500 employees, was up and running.

The secret? Oreck anticipated the worst and had plans in place. Before Katrina hit, the company had transferred its computer operations and call center to backup or continuity locations in Colorado. When the storm hit, it took two days to re-establish lost communications with employees.

Ingenuity played a role at Oreck and virtually every other company in the region. At Oreck, the 15-year-old son of the company's marketing vice president built a basic Web site allowing employees to post messages; and the company established a toll-free number employees could call for information and recorded messages from Tom Oreck.

In the hours and days that followed, everything, from food and shelter to power were needed. Without power, the entire recovery effort was useless—and the Oreck team assigned to find generators found three in Miami, paying $250,000 for them.

Ironically, a year and half later, Oreck announced they would move the plant that survived so well to another part of the United States. "[Sixteen] months later, Oreck is throwing in the towel and moving its manufacturing to Tennessee. The company says it cannot get enough insurance to cover its Mississippi plant, and cannot hire enough skilled workers to replace those who never returned after the storm, mostly because they had nowhere to live.

"'The decision to move this plant was a very difficult one, a very painful one,' said Oreck, the company president. But late last year 'we came to realize that conditions on the Gulf Coast had changed in ways that made doing business here very difficult.'" ("Oreck Comeback Effort Fails After Katrina,"*Kansas City Star*, January 16, 2007)

The labor force in the New Orleans region is 30% smaller than it was prior to Katrina, according to a Brookings Institution study.

And finally—any discussion of Katrina would be incomplete without the mention of early warnings and bureaucracy, concerns prevalent throughout business. For more than ten years, it has been reported, scientists, media and Gulf area leaders had been warning that the day of the big and fatal hurricane was inevitable. Louisiana State University and University of New Orleans scientists had in fact created computer models showing that the impact of a hurricane had the real potential to overwhelm the levees. As *The New Orleans Time-Picayune* reported: "It's a matter of when, not if."

After

While many of the old rules still apply, the events of 9/11 and Katrina suggest additional urgent criteria:

Crisis management must be a full-time responsibility. Part-time, "when-I-get-to-it" assignments fall far short of the magnitude and urgency of the job.

The obvious is worth re-stating: As companies have faced crises over the years, those that have had solid, well-tested response and continuity plans fare better than those without plans.

Throw out the old notions of vulnerability assessment, which called for weighing the probability of each risk a company might face and concentrating on planning for the most probable. If every risk is subjected to the tough questions ("Are we prepared?" and "Can we prevent this?"), then you can have a clear picture of your readiness. As former British Prime Minister Margaret Thatcher once offered: "The unexpected happens. You had better prepare for it."

Plan for business continuity as if your survival depended on it. Dozens of smart companies in the Gulf region were able to continue essential services through alternate locations and to resume operations as quickly as possible.

Regular crisis simulations are enormously helpful and are essential. The results are a disciplined crisis team and the almost certain result that each simulation will lead to an improved procedure or reveal a step which can prevent a real crisis.

But more is needed—and that is a commitment to drills for the crisis team, and evacuation drills for all employees.

When an alarm sounds, the reaction most people seem to have when faced with an emergency is disbelief. This cannot be happening. "Michael Lindell, a Professor at the Hazard Reduction & Recovery Center at Texas A&M University, observed that most people go their entire lives without a disaster. 'So,' he says, 'the most reasonable reaction when something bad happens is to say, "This can't possibly be happening to me."'" He sees the same reaction when large numbers of people are faced with an evacuation. People caught up in disasters tend to fall into three categories. About 10 to 15% remain calm and act quickly and efficiently. Another 14% or less loses control—weeping, screaming or otherwise hindering the evacuation. But the vast majority does very little initially. They are stunned and bewildered." (Amanda Ripley, "How to Get Out Alive," *Time*, May 2, 2005)

Generally accepted standards for crisis management are urgently needed. The thousands of post-9/11, well-meaning guides and the recent push for adaptation of NFPA 1600 (see Chapter 7) are not enough. The time has come for a national crisis institute that will house the standards, provide certifications and training, and act as the clearing house for best practices in crisis management.

And finally, the time has come to hold CEOs accountable for their crisis planning.

Think of how to calm your employees. And leadership counts. On 9/11, the leader was New York's Mayor Rudy Giuliani—whose physical presence and calming, strong words through the days and weeks following 9/11 lifted the spirits of everyone. How? It was his combination of decisiveness, candor and compassion.

When the planes hit the World Trade Center and the horror was seen instantly on TV, businesses across the United States, whether affected or not, needed to calm jittery staffs. As Paul Argenti of Dartmouth College's Tuck School of Business put it, "In periods of upheaval, workers want concrete evidence that top management views their distress as one of the company's key concerns. Written statements have their place, but oral statements and the sound of the empathic human voice communicates sincerity. And if the voice belongs to a company leader, the listener has reason to think that the full weight of the company stands behind whatever promises and assurances are being made. In the words of Rob Densen, Oppenheimer's director of corporate affairs and a survivor of the 1993 bombing of the World Trade Center, most people engulfed in a crisis 'want to be led' and accordingly need to trust that you are going to lead them." ("Crisis

Communications: Lessons from 9/11," Paul Argenti, *Harvard Business Review*, December 1. 2002)

Entergy, the power company in the path of Katrina, offered a "baker's dozen" of lessons learned—and here I am going to break the rule of No More than Three Key Messages (see p. 106), because this is so important.

1. In a crisis, speed is not everything. Speed is the only thing.
2. Create detailed communications plans covering all kinds of crises—and drill them.
3. Have a pre-determined, pre-equipped command center. And get your first troops there fast.
4. Make your own organizational decisions on issues like evacuation.
5. Don't wait for government to act—that may be too late.
6. Enforce "one voice" communications.
7. Assume all normal communications methods will collapse; have backups ready. Toll-free lines and key cell phones need out-of-region area codes.
8. Have lines of authority and approval processes set beforehand. Understand that employees—not customers—are your most important audience.
9. Anticipate significant emotional strain.
10. Good response and good communications go hand in hand—if one fails, they both fail.
11. Take calculated risks—especially in dealing with the media. Abandon your conservatism.
12. Learn from your mistakes.
13. And finally—remember that the more prepared a company is, the less dependent they will be on local government resources, which may be overwhelmed in a disaster.

Change continues. Just a few examples:

The Business Roundtable created a secure telecommunications bridge that enables senior federal officials and CEOs to exchange timely information in the event of a terrorist threat or a crisis. CEO COM LINK[SM] has been expanded to include representatives from the banking, chemicals and water industry sectors, with other critical infrastructure sectors to be added in the future.

Security has been tightened at office buildings and other sites across the US. In an uneven checkerboard of procedures, visitors in some locations are met with procedures that require escorts, while in other locations a signature in the lobby—with no further proof of appointment or ID—is all that is required. The increased demand for security "officers" and the cost of wages and training continues to be a challenge.

Mail is being scanned before delivery throughout some buildings, creating a boom for email and a big question mark about the future of "snail mail." The post-9/11 anthrax scare coincided with a downward spiral for "snail mail" in favor of email, instant messaging and FedEx and UPS.

Insurance against terrorism may also be available.

The Web is our instant news source , while the great divide between the informed and the uninformed public grows, as does cynicism towards mainstream news media.

On a different note, 9/11 created deeper feelings of patriotism.

The Blackout of 2003

Fifty million businesses lost power in the U.S. and Canada in the Blackout of 2003, crippling a huge area of the northeastern and central United States.

New York City's Michael Bloomberg, vowing to avoid another blackout, created a plan for the city that was put to the test during the intense heat of 2006. A crucial part of the post-2003 strategy was the creation of a database of private and government backup generators already in place for a variety of safeguards. When the city's power grid was once again strained in 2006, the government and private entities were told to switch to their standby generators, thus temporarily relieving the Con Ed grid of the pressure.

In addition, the plan called for an ongoing inventory of supplies, so that there would be an orderly distribution should they be needed.

And finally, in a bow to low-tech communications, the neighborhood conservation plan deployed sound trucks and door-to-door visits to large buildings, urging conservation of power with a simple message: raise thermostats during the heat spell and help conserve power.

After

There was no blackout of 2006.

Air Florida

Consider the Air Florida crash of 1982, where 79 passengers perished in a crash into the icy Potomac River shortly after takeoff in a blinding snowstorm. The wings, it turned out, were heavily weighed down by ice and the plane crashed on takeoff.

After

De-icing practices and regulations now are standard.

Exxon Valdez

The *Exxon Valdez* oil spill of nearly 11 million gallons of crude oil became an icon of how not to respond to a crisis. Interestingly, the *Valdez* spill was not one of the biggest (though any spill is serious), but it is remembered in the hall of fame of oil spills as perhaps the most famous because of lack of response and lack of caring. For hours and days of silence, Exxon CEO Lawrence Rawl was conspicuous for his absence and lack of public state-ments of concern. It was rumored that Rawl was suspicious of the media and this affected his decision to avoid the spotlight. Some sources even reported that requests for interviews were met with replies that Rawl had no time for that sort of thing.

After about a week, Frank Iarossi, who ran Exxon Shipping, held a press conference in Valdez, delivering what he thought was some good news about the cleanup—and was immediately contradicted by the media and local fishermen. Amid the communications delays, Iarossi announced that the cleanup was under way, when in fact the only action that had taken place to that point was a boat tour of the area to assess the damage.

When Rawl finally did face the media, it was on live television. When asked about the plans for the cleanup, it was clear he had not read the plans, and stated it was not the job of the chairman to read reports of this type.

While the ship's captain was found to have been intoxicated, Exxon's CEO finally did visit the site—after more than two weeks. Boycotts linger to this day for some customers. Fines and cleanup costs eventually cost the company billions.

Exxon's CEO and senior management, perceived as being aloof and underestimating the problem, suffered lingering criticism remembered more than 15 years later.

Though the bulk of the actual blame for the accident has appropri-ately fallen on the shoulders of ship Captain Ed Hazelwood, investigations have also shown that company-mandated cuts in the size of tanker crews could have been a contributing factor—or at the least could have helped to prevent the accident had the cuts not been enforced. In such situations, smaller crews are overworked and are more prone to fatigue.

On the night of the accident, a local pilot, as is customary, guided the boat out of the port. Hazelwood then left the bridge and went to his cabin. Records show that his departure from the bridge before the ship reached the open ocean was a violation. Add to that another violation: the third mate he assigned to the bridge was not licensed to steer the ship in the coastal waters.

But looking at Hazelwood himself, it was well known on the tanker and in the company that he had an alcohol abuse history. This was especially ironic as he also was known as the best captain in the company's fleet.

After

–Stiffer government regulations and increased spill-prevention requirements and response procedures by Alyeska Pipeline Service, the industry consortium that manages the Valdez port terminal and the 800-mile Trans-Alaska Pipeline, are in place.
–Oil industry safety standards have been tightened, along with emergency response planning.
–Escort tugs now accompany outbound tankers.
–U.S. Coast Guard has increased tracking procedures.
–Ship captains are tested for alcohol and drugs.
–The biggest risk reduction comes from the requirement—mandatory by 2015—that oil tankers must be constructed as double hull vessels, so that should an accident occur and the outer hull is damaged, the oil would be retained between the double walls.

And *Exxon Valdez* is now part of the lexicon of how not to handle a crisis, especially with regard to corporate arrogance and how not to communicate.

False Alarms

An entire book could be devoted to the false alarms and scares of the past few decades. The media and the public have jumped on a number of health-related scares which, after careful analysis, were empty. The Alar scare of 1989 showed how one TV program, *60 Minutes*, could bring the entire apple industry to near ruin when the program reported that the chemical preservative used on apples could cause cancer in children.

Or consider the Harvard research that claimed that two cups of coffee a day doubled the risk of pancreatic cancer, and three cups nearly tripled it. Five years later, the same Harvard group repeated the study and failed to confirm the findings. (Source: Jane Brody, "Health Scares that Weren't So Scary," *The New York Times*, August 18, 1998)

The Alar Scare

The Natural Resources Defense Council organized a public relations campaign claiming that Alar, a chemical sprayed on apples so that they would ripen with some consistency, would cause cancer, and the media responded vigorously. Apples, the American fruit icon, were now forbidden fruit. It was *60 Minutes* that led the pack, with the news that this chemical was a human carcinogen. Public outcry following the media reports forced growers to stop using Alar, and the chemical's manufacturer, Uniroyal, pulled it from the market. And the apple industry was left in shambles.

Subsequent tests by the National Cancer Institute and the Environmental Protection Agency showed no cancer connection. The reality was, according to the International Apple Institute, if there was any threat at all, one would have to eat 28,000 apples a day for a lifetime.

Deny the Problem and the Customers Will Force Change

Intel

In 1994, Intel learned that when a customer is concerned, it is time to pay attention and not minimize the problem. The problem in this case was a flaw in a chip used for mathematical calculating that had the potential for a rare miscalculation—again, a case where the consumer does not want to be or cannot afford to be the one with the failing chip. Intel at first minimized the problem, initially brought to its attention when Thomas Nicely, a mathematician, at Lynchburg College in Virginia, posted a note to a Web site describing how his processor had erred in dividing two fractions. Reports of miscalculations then flowed in through the Web site, while Intel turned its back to the consumer concerns.

Months of public criticism of Intel came to a climax when giant customer IBM cancelled orders for the chips and accused Intel of underestimating the potential for error. After months of increasingly bad publicity, Intel apologized to all customers and offered replacement chips. According to *The Wall Street Journal*: "Investors reacted favorably to Intel's move, sending the company's stock, which had plummeted after the IBM announcement, up $3.4375 to $61.25 a share ... . Analysts said the increase reflected a belief that the episode was now behind Intel, and that it won't badly hurt Intel's earnings or fundamental market position." (Jim Carlton and Stephen Kerider Yoder, "Humble Pie: Intel to Replace its Pentium Chips," *The Wall Street Journal*, December 21, 1994)

In an interview with *The Wall Street Journal*, Intel CEO Andy Grove said: "To some people this seemed arrogant and uncaring. We apologize for that. Intel's old replacement policy was based on an 'Intel-knows-best' attitude ... . We came to the realization that what upset people was, here was Intel making decisions for them." ("Firm Reverses Itself on Pentium Policy," *The Wall Street Journal*, December 21, 1994)

Grove, reflecting in his memoirs: "[M]ost CEOs are in the center or a fortified palace, and news from the outside has to percolate through layers of people from the periphery where the action is ... it took a barrage of relentless criticism to make me realize that something had changed ... . We need to expose ourselves to our customers ... . We need to expose ourselves to lower-level employees who, when encouraged, will tell us. a lot that we need to know. We must invite comments even from people whose job it is to constantly evaluate and criticize us, such as journalists and members of the financial community, as we throw ourselves into raw action, our senses and instincts will rapidly be honed again." (Andrew S. Grove, *Only the Paranoid Survive,* (Currency, 1996) reported in "How We Miscalculated," *Time*, September 2, 1996)

Bureaucracy and Bureaucrats

The Chicago Flood of 1992

An ordinary bureaucratic order to immediately repair a crack in a tunnel under the Chicago River turned into a flood and chaos for downtown Chicago when a city worker ignored the order. The bureaucrat, instead of heeding the urgency of the situation—at a repair cost of approximately $10,000—took the time to get competitive estimates as the crack widened and the tunnel flooded. The acting transportation commissioner was fired, but too late to prevent the huge floods that closed 200 office buildings, knee-deep in water and without power, for days.

Stanford University

After several attempts to be considered for an entry-level accounting position at Stanford were ignored, an accountant finally found a position with the U.S. Government. By coincidence, he was assigned to audit Stanford's government research grants. He found a pattern of unauthorized charges for such items as flowers for the university president's wedding reception and furniture for his home.

While the university quickly hired an independent auditing firm to investigate, correct the problem and install new accounting safeguards, Stanford President Donald Kennedy refused to be contrite, especially when facing a Congressional subcommittee. Shortly after his embarrassing testimony, the Stanford board of trustees asked for his resignation.

White Collar Crimes and Misdeeds

"Many of the crises that have engulfed large public companies in the past several years (A.H. Robbins, Enron, MCI/ WorldCom, Union Carbide, etc.) have been called 'shocking' or 'unexpected.' The fact of the matter is that very few of these occurrences were so unusual, or so unpredictable, that the companies affected could not have taken significant steps to prevent them, or to deal with them much more effectively when their efforts at prevention failed."

—Suzanne Hopgood and Michael W. Tankersley,
Board Leadership for the Company in Crisis
(National Association of Corporate Directors, 2005)

Corporate Shenanigans

Unprecedented financial scandals which harmed helpless shareholders and employees were topped by the collapse of Enron and its auditors, Arthur Andersen. Tyco and WorldCom competed for the headlines as well, all with a common thread: financial hubris, where the senior executives thought they would not be caught. They were caught, and joined their fellow CEOs in jail.

Enron, WorldCom, Tyco, Qwest, and Global Crossing—a few of the more startling financial failures of recent years—destroyed a combined $460 billion in shareholder value.

Hewlett-Packard

And along comes HP, newly refocused and rolling along after the demise of controversial CEO Carly Fiorina—with shocking news that the company's chair, Patricia Dunn, was accused of directing or at least sanctioning investigations of board members who allegedly leaked news to the media. The roots of the problem go back to the highly controversial acquisition of Compaq, a lagging computer maker seen by chair Fiorina as the future of

HP. The board battle, played out in headlines, sowed the seeds for a divided board.

As news of board matters leaked, the company hired private detectives to trail board members and even a star reporter for *The Wall Street Journal*. After an agonizing public display of scrutiny, Dunn was declared innocent at last—though she no longer is board chair.

A.H. Robins & the Dalkon Shield

A.H. Robbins Company, makers of the Dalkon Shield intrauterine birth control device (and a number of famous consumer products such as Robitussin and ChapStick) faced a consumer class action suit claiming that the Dalkon product had caused a number of injuries and deaths. Although the product had been taken off the market years before the class action suit, the litigation revealed that the company had relied on inadequate safety tests and had ignored safety warnings from the product's inventor. The company CEO, fearing the pressure of the media, did not respond to interviews.

Faced with a mountain of lawsuits, the company filed for bankruptcy and eventually sold its famous brands.

Enron and Arthur Andersen Go Down in Flames

Massive energy trader Enron shocked the world with its collapse, falling like dominoes. "Enron's fatal flaw," according to *Time* magazine "was management hubris, tacitly encouraged by board members, regulators, politicians and stock analysts—many with financial ties to Enron—who looked the other way as warning lights began to flash. Feeling it could do no wrong, the company too often pursued unprofitable markets, obscured the costs and stiff-armed anyone who asked for an explanation." (Daniel Kadlec, "Power Failure," *Time*, December 10, 2001) Within a year of the breaking news, the company's stock lost 99% of its value. Innocent shareholders, including thousands of employees, lost billions.

The failures were compounded by evidence that Enron's auditors, the once-venerable Arthur Andersen accounting firm, had instructed staff members to destroy Enron audit materials, thus obstructing the government's investigation of fraud at Enron—making it very difficult to untangle the web of Enron's creation of partnerships with shell companies, the creation of which made many Enron executives rich. The scandal brought Arthur Andersen to an untimely grave as well.

Tyco International

In the golden days of Dennis Kozlowski, a visit to Tyco International's headquarters on Manhattan's 57th Street was more like visiting a museum of antiquities. Perched on a high floor, with sweeping views of Central Park, Tyco's offices bore no evidence of its diverse businesses or any credo. Antique rugs, precious Old World oil paintings and the resident chef and wandering shoeshine lady gave the impression of a fine way of life at Tyco.

Kozlowski commuted between the company's modest New Hampshire office, the sunny high rise in Boca Raton, Florida, and his yacht *Endeavor*. At its most frantic pace of acquisitions, in 2000, it was reported that the company acquired in the neighborhood of 365 companies—the equivalent of an acquisition a day.

The empire came crashing down when Kozlowski was found to have avoided local sales tax by shipping empty boxes to his New Hampshire address, while the actual art was delivered to his Manhattan address. In a rapid succession of investigations, Kozlowski and his close deputies were found to have used hundreds of millions of dollars of company funds for personal purposes. Kozlowski and his former CFO are serving prison terms.

Bewildered Consumers

Ford/Firestone

In one of the most unusual crises—this involving two corporations battling each other in public—Ford Motor Company and Firestone Tires provided an ideal story for the media's appetite for the sensational.

When Ford discovered that a certain model of Firestone tire widely used on the popular Explorer model was defective, the missteps began. At first, Firestone announced they would immediately recall the tires in South America, because the problem was first discovered in Venezuela. They would get around to the rest of the hemisphere later. This did not sit well with U.S. consumers, who feared the worst. When Firestone announced free replacements of tires for everyone, consumers were shocked to find that, when they appeared at the dealers, the dealers knew nothing about the offer.

In the end, not only did Ford stop using the tires, but General Motors and Nissan curtailed their use as well.

Amid the public accusations of mismanagement flying between Ford and Firestone, it was clear that the public was quickly losing confidence because there was no assurance of an adequate supply of replacement tires. Promises of investigations were not sufficient. The public wanted new tires and they wanted them immediately.

In the end, the company with the most at stake in the crisis, Firestone, was the most graphic failure, for they did not put customer safety first and were clearly unprepared to handle the most rudimentary aspects of the crisis—communications and logistics.

Pet Food Recall

In early 2007, devoted pet owners across the United States became concerned about the news of contaminated dog and cat food. As several pet deaths were reported, the list of affected brands grew almost daily. The brand manufacturers were as much the victims as the pets and their owners. Blame went to the supplier of raw materials, Canada's Menu Foods. In turn, accusations flew across the globe to China, where some of the raw materials originated. Brand by brand, products were recalled while the blame continued to circulate. The issue here is how to pinpoint blame in a complex supply chain—a tough question to answer while the public worries and suffers.

Attacks and Fraud in Cyberspace

The 21st century began with a crime unheard of just a decade earlier. Jonathan Leber, a 15-year-old New Jersey teenager, made nearly $275,000 in profits as the result of posting bogus information in chat rooms, driving up the price of various stocks in his portfolio. Leber became the first minor to ever be charged by the SEC with securities fraud. Though the crime was nothing new, the stunning reality was that it has been made simple by the existence of the PC and the Web.

How Bad Can It Get?

Union Carbide

In December 1984, 2000 people died when a Bhopal, India, chemical plant, owned 51% by Union Carbide, released a poison gas, methyl isocyanate (MIC). Another 100,000 to 200,000 people were blinded or otherwise injured.

The accident was the result of improper procedures, improper training and slow reactions to warnings. Here was another example of a small problem escalating into disaster. When the initial leak was found, maintenance workers decided to wait until after their tea break to fix it. And when the alarms were sounded to warn of the break in the system, many workers ignored them—some thinking it was a drill.

When a similar incident at their Institute, West Virginia, plant occurred, Union Carbide first denied any similarities between the two releases, even hinting at sabotage. Trying to ease community concern, the company conducted a community town meeting, only to be fiercely criticized by angry and frightened neighbors. Only later did the company admit to multiple shortcomings in the operations.

After

The two events and the company's response had far-reaching implications for Union Carbide, whose chairman admitted that the company did not have a crisis plan. The CEO lost his job, and the company was ultimately acquired by a competitor.

The crisis has had far-reaching affects beyond Union Carbide as well. The Union Carbide tragedies and the media attention they received placed communities around the world, especially those with chemical plants in the backyards, on edge, while the chemical industry began taking a fresh look at community safety.

Three Mile Island Accident

The handling of the "meltdown" at Pennsylvania's Three Mile Island Nuclear power plant in 1979, just a few years prior to the Tylenol scare, had a major negative impact on the nuclear industry, and serves as a textbook case for how not to handle a crisis. The facility was unprepared to communicate with the public and calm their fears, and so the nationwide fear of a nuclear disaster arose. In the aftermath of the scare, nuclear power advocates began an extensive media campaign to convince the public that we need nuclear power and that it is safe. The campaign is a classic example of the wrong way to communicate risk to the public, including a public service announcement in which an actor portraying a scientist stood on the steps of the Lincoln Memorial and proclaimed (with no other explanation) that there is more radiation coming from the limestone in the Memorial than from Three Mile Island. And what was the public's reaction? A continued distrust of the nuclear energy industry, and a potential new-found fear of visiting the Lincoln Memorial. A savvy public ignored the message.

Trapped on the Tarmac

Stories of airplanes stuck for hours on the tarmac in bad weather, filled to capacity with irate passengers, are not new, as Northwest Airlines and others made headlines several years ago. In the Northwest case, a determined passenger, using his cell phone, finally was able reach the airline CEO at home, and then action was taken. More recently, an American Airlines pilot, tired of standing on the tarmac, finally moved the plane to an empty gate despite lack of authorization to do so.

One would have thought these crises would have taught other airlines lessons.

In February 2007, amid several days of icy weather, the old problems plagued JetBlue, bringing the company to its knees. Combine ice and snow and a good dose of well-intentioned play-by-the-book bureaucracy and JetBlue, known for its service, suddenly was in crisis.

Some waits on the tarmac—only to fly nowhere—were up to 8 hours, as toilets overflowed and passengers grew more and more agitated and hungry—wondering why buses could not be brought to the planes and everyone brought safely to the terminals.

Apologies have come from the airlines, with promises these incidents will not be repeated. This is an example of crisis resolution in progress, as passengers push for a congressionally mandated passenger bill of rights which would impose financial penalties on the airlines for incidents of this type. The airlines, meanwhile, continue to fight the legislation, with promises of voluntary compliance. JetBlue's CEO has been quick to apologize to the customers and announce new procedures and a passenger bill of rights. In a national newspaper advertising campaign in February 2007, David Neeleman, JetBlue's chairman, said:

"Words cannot express how truly sorry we are for the anxiety, frustration and inconvenience that you, your family, friends and colleagues experienced. This is especially saddening because JetBlue was founded on the promise of bringing humanity back to air travel, and making the experience of flying happier and easier for everyone who chooses to fly with us. We know we failed to deliver on this promise last week."

Neeleman then issued a first-ever Bill of Rights for Airline Passengers.

Wall Street reacted well to the apologies and the Bill of Rights. "We believe that JetBlue's PR efforts since the last weekend have been rather successful at expressing humility and embarrassment about the problems," wrote Morgan Stanley analyst William J. Greene in a note to clients. "This *mea culpa* has likely gone a long way to mitigate customer frustrations."

Rarely has a company created a specific set of promises so quickly, in response to a crisis. The Bill of Rights is worth noting as a benchmark:

INFORMATION

JetBlue will notify customers of the following:

> Delays prior to scheduled departure
> Cancellations and their cause
> Diversions and their cause

CANCELLATIONS

All customers whose flight is cancelled by JetBlue will, at the customer's option, receive a full refund or reservation on a future JetBlue flight at no additional charge or fare. If JetBlue cancels a flight within 12 hours of scheduled departure and the cancellation is due to a Controllable Irregularity, JetBlue will also provide the customer with a Voucher valid for future travel on JetBlue in the amount paid to JetBlue for the customer's roundtrip.

DEPARTURE DELAYS

Customers whose flight is delayed prior to scheduled departure for 1-2 hours due to a Controllable Irregularity are entitled to a $25 Voucher good for future travel on JetBlue.

Customers whose flight is delayed prior to scheduled departure for 2-4 hours due to a Controllable Irregularity are entitled to a $50 Voucher good for future travel on JetBlue.

Customers whose flight is delayed prior to scheduled departure for 4-6 hours due to a Controllable Irregularity are entitled to a Voucher good for future travel on JetBlue in the amount paid by the customer for the one-way trip.

Customers whose flight is delayed prior to scheduled departure for more than 6 hours due to a Controllable Irregularity are entitled to a Voucher good for future travel on JetBlue in the amount paid by the customer for the roundtrip.

OVERBOOKINGS

Customers who are involuntarily denied boarding shall receive $1,000.

GROUND DELAYS

For customers who experience a Ground Delay for more than 5 hours, JetBlue will take necessary action so that customers may deplane.

JetBlue will also provide customers experiencing a Ground Delay with food and drink, access to restrooms and, as necessary, medical treatment.

ARRIVALS

Customers who experience a Ground Delay on Arrival for 30-60 minutes are entitled to a $25 Voucher good for future travel on JetBlue.

Customers who experience a Ground Delay on Arrival for 1-2 hours are entitled to a $100 Voucher good for future travel on JetBlue.

Customers who experience a Ground Delay on Arrival for 2-3 hours are entitled to a Voucher good for future travel on JetBlue in the amount paid by the customer for the one-way trip.

Customers who experience a Ground Delay on Arrival for more than 3 hours are entitled to a Voucher good for future travel on JetBlue in the amount paid by the customer for the roundtrip.

DEPARTURES:

Customers who experience a Ground Delay on Departure for 3-4 hours are entitled to a $100 Voucher good for future travel on JetBlue.

Customers who experience a Ground Delay on Departure for more than 4 hours are entitled to a Voucher good for future travel on JetBlue in the amount paid by the customer for the roundtrip.

* * *

4   Denial in the Land of Risk

B efore 9/11, many Americans—and American businesses—thought of disasters as fires, explosions and natural phenomena. It is fair to say that 9/11 reached our collective psyches. Despite considerable efforts to encourage individuals and businesses to prepare for the new age of calamities, America remains woefully unprepared. The Council for Excellence in Government listed the top concerns among the American public:

–76% of U.S. adults believe there will be another terrorist attack.

–50% of U.S. adults think the attack may be near where they live or work.

–About 67% of U.S. adults say they would volunteer their time to get trained to help, but they need to know how.
(Source: "U.S. Public Unprepared, *The Wirthlin Report*, December 2004)

But, Wirthlin continues, "[M]ost do not walk the walk. While Americans recognize the importance of being personally prepared, fewer than two in ten U.S. adults characterize themselves as very prepared ... and findings show that most Americans feel their employers and their children's schools are still behind the curve. In fact, half of U.S. adults say their employers have not provided them with any information or training on a disaster/emergency plan."

This last observation identifies a shocking gap between the claims that companies say their most important asset is their people, and the reality. Even a rudimentary plan is worth sharing with employees. And, in this same context, the more businesses are able to sort out the Tower of Babble on personal advice, the better off the employees will be.

The Economist has created a Corporate Risk Barometer, which looks at what corporate risk managers consider their primary concerns. In 2005, they listed reputational risk and regulatory risk at the top. The third most significant threat was IT network security branches and systems failure. (Source: "Businesses Feel More at Risk," **Continuity Central**, April 15, 2005)

Several myths or excuses stand in the way of business preparedness

Excuse #1

It's expensive to create a plan.

Fact: Yes, it costs money, but that expense is negligible compared to the cost of recovering from a crisis that could have been prevented or managed so that the losses and disruptions were minimal. The cost associated with a mismanaged crisis is far more than the actual expense of destroyed goods or idled labor. A company's most precious asset—its reputation, built carefully over the years—is on the line, too. It takes only one poorly managed crisis to send a company into a reputation tailspin from which it may never recover.

Nonetheless, economic shortsightedness continues to prevail in some quarters. "Left to their own devices, companies simply will not make the needed [security] investments," says Peter Navarro, economist at the University of California at Irvine. "That's the grim reality." ("Post-9/11: How Corporate America Responds," **Travel Vault**, National Business Travelers Association, undated)

Excuse #2

It won't happen here. Who cares about my company? We make boring products in an out of the way place.

Fact: The first reaction in many crises is denial—this cannot be happening. On any given day, bad things happen to good companies. Everything from tornadoes to employee violence to acts of terrorism darkens the doors of companies every day around the globe. And here's a surprising statistic: 91% of us live in areas that are considered high risk.

"Historically, humans get serious about avoiding disasters only after one has just smacked them in the face," notes **Time** magazine. "[A] review of the past year in disaster history suggests that modern Americans are particularly, mysteriously bad at protecting themselves from guaranteed threats. We know more than we ever did about the dangers we face. But it turns out that in times of crisis, our greatest enemy is rarely the storm, the quake or the surge itself. More often, it is ourselves." (Amanda Ripley, "Floods, Tornadoes, Hurricanes, Wildfire, Earthquakes ... Why We Don't Prepare," *Time*, August 28, 2006)

Denial is not new in our society. Look at some of the nagging, chronic issues we face, such as problems of the homeless, or the issue of universal health care for all Americans. These and other problems have not reached crisis proportions, and so we work at the edges of the problems but find no resolution. When we are in a fight for survival, however, we know how to act and to act fast. When we realized we needed to end World War II, the Manhattan Project was launched and the atomic bomb was developed at breakneck speed. Though the events of 9/11 in particular have led to protective changes, they are not enough.

Excuse #3

There is little proof or information about terrorist threats. So why should I get all worked up about the next terrorist attack?

Fact: There is ample evidence of terrorist activity around the world, even though official government sources can say very little. The war against terrorism is like no other, given the lack of contact with any leadership and the dispersed army of terrorists.

Excuse #4

There is no correlation between crisis preparation and stock price—which, after all, is all that matters.

Fact: Wall Street does not like uncertainty—especially one not addressed head-on—because there is enough uncertainty on Wall Street already.
Wall Street punishes companies in crisis—and it happens quickly. Recovery to the pre-crisis level is a big challenge for some companies. While many recover, many others do not.

Excuse #5

Planning is complicated and time consuming, and we just cannot afford the distraction.

Fact: You cannot afford not to. Once companies accept crisis planning as a normal part of their business, it becomes just that—a normal part of business. The more routine a company makes crisis planning, the more accepted and efficient it becomes, and the more protected your company is from the unexpected.

Excuse #6

I understand that once the plan's in place, we need to train our people. And if that's not enough, I hear we need to do periodic simulations. There is no way we can take the time!

Fact: Training, like all other aspects of crisis planning, can and should become a part of the company's routine. Simulations, whether annual or semi-annual, are unusual and do disrupt the company routines for the time they take. The most effective ones do not exceed four hours plus another hour or two for debriefing to discuss lessons learned and steps to take to improve. (The big war games you hear about are important, but leave those to the government agencies.)

There's an interesting plus to the simulations, which I have noticed over the years. A company invariably discovers during a simulation a previously overlooked area of operations that, if corrected, may prevent a crisis. It doesn't get much better than that.

The bottom line is simple. Every day spent in denial is a day a company places itself deeper into risky waters.

If your company needs further motivation, consider the competitive advantage of joining those companies that work every day to improve their crisis preparedness and leaving your competitors in the ranks of the unprepared. And if nothing else motivates you to work on a crisis plan for your company on a calm day, then you may want to get to work on the explanations you will need to deliver to boards, shareholders, customers, government investigators and the media in the midst of a crisis explaining why you were not prepared.

Excuse #7

Crises will happen, and there's nothing much you can do except wait for them to happen and then roll with the punches.

Fact: Many situations can be spotted before they become crises—if the right prevention and issue-management systems are in place.

Excuse #8

It's all about managing our reputation when a crisis hits. And we'll leave that to our PR department to take care of.

Fact: The PR department is a key component of every crisis plan and team. But the best PR people are not simply spin doctors. They are communications strategists and implementers. And they are able to tell, for example, about the actions being taken to resolve the crisis. The entire team needs to work on those actions.

Excuse #9

It's almost impossible to know where to start when looking for generally accepted rules for planning

Fact: How true! Since 9/11 the Web has been filled with a Tower of Babble of guidance and information from the U.S. government, the American Red Cross, and virtually every professional and trade association. Most of it is quite good, but the abundance of all of this information—without some ranking or analysis by a business equivalent of *Consumer Reports* leaves planners adrift. All the while, the much-touted NFPA1600 lurks around the edges as an attempted official guidepost. This document, drawn up by the National Fire Protection Association, is an exhaustive checklist for mid-level crisis managers.

Excuse #10

No one made me prepare.

Fact: Does your board care about the company's reputation? If they do, they should include, high on the governance list, the oversight for the company's crisis prevention and readiness plans.

Norman Augustine, former CEO of Lockheed Martin, put it very well in "How to Turn a Crisis into a Catastrophe in 12 Easy Steps."

Assume the evidence of the problem must be wrong.
When evidence mounts, cover up the problem.
Let the lawyers manage the response strategy—admit nothing.
When the problem becomes public, minimize it.
Never display remorse; blame someone else, preferably the victim.
Take plenty of time to study the problem.

Have the highest-level responsible individual go into hiding.
Attack the media.
Anger the regulators, preferably by embracing untenable positions.
Shift the spotlight to the failing of the regulators.
Frequently reverse your position and contradict yourself.
Give priority to saving money on the front end—that way you have more
to lose later.

　　　—"Report of the National Association of Corporate Directors
　　　　　　　Blue Ribbon Commission on Risk Oversight"
　　　　　　　　　　　　Norman Augustine, 2002

Excuse #11

In a disaster, the government will take over and manage everything. So
why should our company bother with a crisis plan?

Fact: The government cannot and will not do everything. While it
appears that reforms have been put in place since the government mal-
function in the aftermath of Hurricane Katrina, do not expect the government to be all-compassing in its management of a disaster. As George
Foresman, Undersecretary for the Department of Homeland Security's
Preparedness Directorate put it:

　　　"Government will be able to do as much as it can reasonably do in
the aftermath of an emergency or disaster. But we have not built our government structures nor does business have a motivational incentive to con-
struct our systems and our processes to be able to deal with a full range of
emergencies and disasters that potentially will confront this nation. In other
words, we're not going to always have shelter for 1.8 million people at the
ready, ready to flip a switch to turn it on.

　　　"We are not going to have in place transportation resources that
could quickly, in 24 hours or less, move hundreds of thousands people from
a major metropolitan area to other areas in the aftermath of an emergency
or disaster." (Address by George Foresman to the US Chamber of Com-
merce, June 1, 2006, Washington D.C.)

　　　The simple, most difficult reality is that we do not know when or
where the next act of terrorism or any other crisis may occur, but we can be
prepared to deal with it effectively, if we remember all the details—including the "I forgots."

　　　An examination of how to avoid some of the most common omis-
sions can help keep any company on the road to continuous improvement
and readiness:

(1) **Find the crisis plan.** Is the plan easily accessible? Does everyone have a copy? When you need the basics, including the checklists for what everyone needs to remember to do, there is no time for hunting through the shelves and computer files. Where are the phone numbers for key personnel? Where are the e-mail addresses? The best advice: Keep the crisis plan short, preferably on a folded card that fits in a pocket or briefcase. Keep it updated with all the vital contact information. And keep at least one copy of the names and numbers in your wallet or briefcase.

(2) **Take the annual checkup.** Ordinary change is a constant threat to your crisis plan. Personnel turnover can be a major problem. You've got to monitor staff changes and train new members of the crisis teams. A more complex problem comes when businesses and their infrastructures grow or consolidate. This is where crisis plans can easily be forgotten. No company should ever permit a merger or acquisition to relegate the crisis plan to the "forgotten" bin. The best advice: Schedule your annual crisis plan review soon, and stick with it.

(3) **Designate backups.** Who is traveling, on vacation, or out sick? Inevitably, someone on the crisis team is not available when the worst hits. The best advice: Designate backups for every position—and make sure they all are all up to speed on how to perform the job.

(4) **Remember that employees are important.** Do you have a system in place to quickly determine the whereabouts and safety of every employee—at the plant, at the office, at off-site meetings and while traveling? Do you have emergency food and other supplies on hand in the event of a shelter-in-place situation? Do you have flashlights and other evacuation aids on hand in some ready-to-use kits? And do you have a communication system in place to ensure that employees are notified of crisis news as quickly and directly as possible so they do not hear it first on TV or radio broadcasts—or via frantic phone calls from loved ones? The best advice: Don't wait. Put the right tracking system in place as soon as possible.

(5) **Commit to practice, practice, and more practice.** All too often practice sessions are postponed for budget or scheduling reasons. Or they are forgotten altogether. These sessions are invaluable, even critical, reminders of what needs to be done through real-world practice. Inevitably, simulations have tangible results because they identify areas

that need fixing or improvement to either prevent or better manage a crisis.

* * *

5   It's About Leadership and Communication

" **I** do solemnly pledge to uphold and protect the reputation of this corporation and all its brands. In fact, the buck stops here."

Make no mistake—you are in the biggest fishbowl ever seen. When disaster strikes, the eyes of the media will be on you. And you avoid these eyes at your peril.

At the end of the day, it is the reputation of the brand or the company or both that are at stake in a crisis. What is this intangible asset called reputation? Well, it is the total of what various people think about your company or brands or both. Would they buy shares in the company? Would they buy the products over the competitors'? Would they come to work at your company if you offered them a job?

Most CEOs, when asked who is responsible for the reputation of their company, say it is theirs. If reputation is to be preserved in a crisis, a rock-solid, tested crisis prevention and response plan is essential to that responsibility.

But who gets it and who does not?

Which one are you?

There are the **visionaries**—the CEOs in the small, medium and large companies who know that crisis preparation pays. They're still in the minority.

Others are in denial. Let's call them the **avoiders**—the ones who say, "It won't happen here. And by the way, the expense of crisis readiness is an easy expense to cut. After all, no one's really going to hold me accountable"—unless it hits the fan.

Then there are the **vulnerables**—the companies in high-risk industries or high-risk locations that are so well prepared they beat all odds and become the heroes when a worst-case disaster strikes. The most recent examples are those that survived when hurricane Katrina and then hurricane Rita struck the Gulf region in the worst natural disaster our country has ever faced.

According to Ambassador L. Paul Bremer III, "Large corporations can expect to face a crisis on average every four or five years ... [E]very CEO will probably have to manage at least one crisis during their tenure. A director may face two or three crises during a normal tour of service on a board." (L. Paul Bremer III, "Corporate Governance and Crisis Management," *Director and Boards*, Winter, 2002)

Mistakes and crises will occur. You and the company will be judged not on the mistakes, but on what you have done about them—specifically, what steps have been taken to prevent the same problem.

The Power of the CEO

Are there executive patterns that create crises and lead to the downfall of the CEO?

The Home Depot
Enron
Tyco
BP
Hewlett-Packard

Hubris seems to connect them all. But there are other traits. Management experts have pointed to a few traits evident in many CEOs who go off the deep end, including:

Poor Self-Image

Some simply want to bury their humble beginnings, according to Jeffrey Sonnenfeld, associate dean at the Yale School of Management. "They were so desperate to define themselves by what they weren't," says Sonnenfeld, "that they forgot who they were." (Source: Bruce Horowitz, "Scandals Grow Out of CEOs' Warped Mind-Set," *USA Today*, October 11, 2002)

"I deserve it"

After all, I've led this company to the great success it is.

You have been anointed

A few months before Dennis Kozlowski was arrested for tax fraud, *Business Week* named him one of the top 25 managers of the year.

"Some are, according to experts, simply bored or lonesome. And there's the age-old tendency for some leaders to lose entire sight of who they are and become unable to separate what is rightfully theirs from what is not, according to Sonnenfeld. Power corrupts." (Bruce Horowitz, "Scandals Grow Out of CEOs' Warped Mind-Set")

Executive power has the capacity for effective crisis planning, too

You can put together the best plan, train the staff and wait. Then, when you thought you've got the best plan to prevent the worst from happening, it happens anyway. And it can happen—because even the best of plans cannot govern the far-flung reaches of today's global corporation. Faced with the challenge of managing from afar, here are a few hints that can help to minimize these problems:

Visit
Communicate
Share plans and updates constantly
Listen
Reward

According to Wayne A. Hochwarter, associate professor of management at Florida State University's College of Business, "[C]risis planning…and sharing the plans with employees…has a substantial affect on worker attitudes:

–Significantly higher levels of job satisfaction
–Greater willingness to do things beyond what is expected by management
–Perception of greater control
–More enthusiasm and a greater willingness to work harder than expected
–More compassion for others
–Greater feelings of support from the organization
–Increase in employees' sense of importance and a building of camaraderie.
–Lower levels of depressed mood at work
(Source: "Research Identifies an Intrinsic Benefit of Continuity Planning," *Continuity Central*, September 6, 2006)

"From Churchill to Giuliani, the leaders who are most effective in crisis are most visible. Whether in person or via other means of communication, leaders must appear engaged, available and in touch. The temptation, or even the necessity, to stay in the office revising budgets and hashing out strategy must be balanced with the need to connect directly with staff, constituents, customers and others who expect to see their leaders in action.

Effective leaders in challenging situations also demonstrate optimism that the challenge will be met successfully but do not downplay the difficulties. Leaders should keep in mind that that fear and pessimism are contagious, particularly when they come from those in charge. At the same time, leaders who sugarcoat bad news or dismiss the obstacles lose credibility." (Wick Keating, "Does History Provide any Guidance?" *Catalyst*, Winter, 2002)

If and when a crisis strikes, when does the CEO speak? Or does the CEO speak? There is growing recognition that the public persona and public conduct of the CEO is a primary factor for success. As recently as 1999, *Fortune* listed the Six Habits of Highly Ineffective CEOs:

–People problems
–Decision gridlock
–Life syndrome
–Bad earnings news
–Missing in action
–Off-the-deep-end financials
(Ram Charan and Geoffrey Colvin, "Why CEOs Fail,"
Fortune, June 21, 1999)

Nowhere was there mention of public persona. Who cared, it would seem, about charisma and communication skills?

Jump to 2006, when *The Wall Street Journal* compared GE's successor to the iconic Jack Welch, Jeff Immelt, with the guy who lost, Bob Nardelli. Nardelli went on to become CEO of Home Depot, then was fired in 2007.

"Messrs. Nardelli and Immelt are the Cain and Abel of the corporate world—both groomed for greatness by Mr. Welch but divided when their mentor had to choose. Mr. Immelt is tall and smooth, a graduate of Dartmouth and Harvard. Mr. Nardelli is short and gruff, with degrees from Western Illinois and Louisville universities … [F]or better or worse it is a much more public game, involving a wide range of constituencies and requiring the skills of a politician." (Alan Murray, "A Tale of Two CEOs:

How Public Perception Shapes Reputations", *The Wall Street Journal*, July 13, 2006)

Is it that simple? What do we really mean when we talk about communication skills and persona as critical attributes? Yes, they are critical— but they do not stand alone. They are part of a complex of factors that, over the years, have evolved despite changing fashions in management.

What, then, are the attributes of an effective CEO, once we strip away the fads and the pontifications of management gurus?

He or she:

–Knows that failures provide great management lessons. (Just don't repeat the same mistake twice.) A crisis may be the greatest test for the CEO and even the life of the brand or the company.

–Knows that leadership involves equal parts of decisiveness and listening. According to the late Peter Drucker, "The issues facing management don't change from year to year. The answers do. The biggest skill needed to address these issues is not really a skill—it is a basic attitude, a willingness to start not with the question 'What do I want to do?' but with the question 'What needs to be done?' It was the willingness to ask this question that made the fairly mediocre Harry Truman a great president and the superbly gifted Richard Nixon a failure." (Michael V. Copeland, "How to Succeed in 2005," *Business 2.0*, December 2004)

–Appreciates, respects and mentors subordinates

–Understands the role of the board—as stewards and strategists

–Is scrupulously honest and has earned the trust of employees and customers. As J & J's Jim Burke said: "If you run a public company, you cannot ignore the public. Institutional trust is far more important than most people realize. The operative word is trust ... and whether people will take one's word when one badly needs them to do so will depend on how much confidence has been built in the organization over the years before the crisis occurs." (Source: Norman R. Augustine, "Managing the Crisis You Tried to Prevent")

–Understands that the public expects and respects transparency. As reputation expert Peter Sandman reminds us, "Transparency is important these days on its own merits, but as a practical matter, it's a better investment for businesses than for politicians. The rule of thumb in business is this: If you know you've got a problem, and you blow the whistle on yourself, you'll do some damage, but only 1/20 the damage that is done if somebody else blows the whistle on you. Secrecy is still a bad investment," adds Sandman. "Customers, not to mention potential whistleblowers inside an organization, have more ways than ever to get information and publicize it." (Peter Sandman, "During Crises, Sandman Says, Politics and Government are Separate Spheres," *Impact*, January, 2007)

–Is a superb communicator—to employees, customers, investors, and the media. Wondering how much to say? Warren Buffet's advice is clear: "First, state clearly that you do not know all the facts. Then promptly state the facts you do know. One's objective should be to get it right, get it quick, get it out, and get it over. You see, your problem won't improve with age."
(Source: Norman R. Augustine, "Managing the Crisis You Tried to Prevent, *Harvard Business Review*, November-December, 1995)

A crisis is a time when the CEO must make it clear that he or she is in charge. While it may seem obvious, it is important to assert this leadership quickly and clearly.

"GE's Jeff Immelt, who has won praise for his management style, offers some criteria that apply to crisis management:

"Simplify constantly. Stay true to your own style. 'Every morning,' says Immelt, 'I look in the mirror and say, "I could have done three things better yesterday ... "'

"And 'Leave a few things unsaid. I may know an answer, but I'll often let the team find its own way. Sometimes, being an active listener is much more effective than ending a meeting with me enumerating 17 actions.'" (John A. Byme, "Practicing More than Jack Preached," *Fast Company*, April 2004)

–Has high energy, and knows how to balance that energy between the job and personal life. "The first essential trait of leadership, according to Jack and Suzy Welch, is positive energy—the capacity to go-go-go with healthy vigor and an upbeat attitude toward good times and bad. The second is the ability to energize others, releasing their positive energy, to take any hill. The third trait is edge—the ability to make tough calls, to say yes or no, not maybe. The fourth trait is the talent to execute—very simply, to get things done. Fifth and finally, leaders have passion. They care deeply. They sweat; they believe." (Jack Welch and Suzy Welch, *Winning* (HarperCollins, 2005)

—Knows how to balance time in a crisis—especially the early hours or days when confusion is more common than order. The CEO, who is the presumed crisis team leader, needs to manage time so that morale is maintained; the media are fed; and a strategy is developed.

Peter Drucker, the late management guru, gave some advice on managing CEO time:

"[I]t is my observation that effective executives do have in common certain practices or habits—and practices can be learned. One obvious practice is the conservation of time. In a peculiar way the executive's time is everybody else's time but his own. Everybody can move in on him, and usually every body does. He cannot shut himself off from these demands, but he must use the little time he can control to do the important things. This is the secret of those few people who accomplish so much with so little apparent effort. They put first things first." (Peter Drucker, "Advice From the Master," *Fortune*, December 12, 2005)

The early moments of a crisis may leave you, the CEO, in a state of mental gridlock. You want to avoid panic at all costs, because panic often leads to closed minds and snap decisions.

Think of a way to step aside in a quiet place to think the situation through; whatever works for you.

But it is not all about you.

—Has the right people on the crisis team. And the best team includes those who are confident to voice their opinions, get things done, and stay focused.

—Remembers that the best spokespersons prepare to face the media. Always have some coaching/rehearsal time before the media invasion.

—Has a strong understanding of and commitment to crisis prevention, preparation and response. And when it does hit the fan, is ready and able to remain calm and direct the company toward fast response.

—Is willing to take responsible risks, recognizing the risk/benefit ratios— which are subjective—and the consequences for brand and company reputation, the balance sheet and share price.

—Believes that the following three points will guide the way:

(1) Crisis readiness is not a sometimes thing, relegated to a security or facilities officer. It is a primary corporate function, managed by a senior company officer who reports directly to the CEO.
(2) The only valid crisis plan is a short one that fits into your pocket or your wallet.
(3) A commitment to several simulations a year is an immovable commitment that yields the benefits of increased readiness and the bonus of discovering actions to continuously improve readiness or in fact to prevent some crises.

–Resists bureaucracy

–Is ready—really ready—to hear bad news

–Has the loyalty of key employees. In fact, it has been said that the true test of a leader is the number of employees who would follow him/her out the door to a new and possibly uncharted new venture.

–Listens to the latest one-size-fits-all management fad, and then considers the value carefully before committing to it.

–Is up to date on what the competition is doing.

–Understands and is able to balance the often conflicting advice of the lawyers and the communicators.

There has been debate for years over who has the upper hand in communicating during a crisis—the corporate communications department or the legal department. The CEO and the crisis team need to face this dilemma. Most lawyers will advocate saying as little as possible, and the communicators will want to communicate as much as possible. If the facts are concrete, there is a great deal to be gained by communicating openly and quickly—in fact, it may save lives and brand reputation.

These lawyer vs. communicator conflicts can be minimized by coming to terms on ground rules in advance of a crisis, and incorporating those ground rules into the crisis plan.

While we are on the subject of the lawyers, we need to recognize that lawyers often are the first to know of an issue or brewing problem that may escalate into a crisis. It is in the best interests of everyone to include the communicators as early as possible. Here are ten indicators that lawyers ought to bring in the communicators:

(1) The media are knocking at the door.
(2) Rumors are afloat.
(3) Some employees know about the problem, and others surely will know soon.
(4) It will take time and intense effort to put a communications strategy, key messages and action plan in place.
(5) The CEO and other key personnel need to be coached and trained to act as the spokespersons.
(6) Third party spokespersons will be crucial allies when or if the issue becomes public—and they will need to be identified.
(7) The company is publicly traded, and news of the problem has the potential to affect share price.
(8) News may leak at any time.
(9) You've never met the communications staff or outside consultants, and they do not have a clue on the issue.
(10) The company or brand reputation is potentially at stake.

–Knows there are times when it is advisable to admit mistakes and apologize.

More on Apologies

It may take 15 seconds to deliver an apology. But an arrogant statement or lack of apology or contrition may require 15 years for recovery. When a CEO or other senior executive communicates in a crisis, there is often the question of whether or not to apologize and when. An apology, according to the American Heritage Dictionary, is "an acknowledgment expressing regret or asking pardon for a fault or offense."

While some lawyers are cautious about the implications of apologizing for a crisis, there is a growing school of thought that an apology or some form of expression of regret over a crisis and all of its affects has a proper place in how a leader communicates in a crisis.

[T]he apology as a form of social exchange is growing in international importance. While the methods may differ—China has apology companies that employ surrogates to provide explanations and express remorse—the apology culture is a global phenomenon." (Barbara Kellerman, "When Should a Leader Apologize and When Not?" *Harvard Business Review*, April, 2006)

When carefully worded to avoid liability or premature admissions of guilt before the facts behind a crisis are determined, there is a great deal to be said for expressions of sympathy, empathy, and concern.

Consider that an apology does the following things:

(1) Calms the agitated customers. Look at a situation we all have faced: a flight delay. The gate agent changes the departure board to show a 90-minute delay, then disappears. Anger mounts, rumors circulate. Now consider another agent who, on posting the new time, makes an announcement: "We apologize for the delay. Weather in Chicago has delayed the arrival of inbound aircraft, but it should be here in 60 minutes. The weather forecast in Chicago is looking quite good now, and we should be ready to leave in 90 minutes. Thanks for your patience." You now know the situation, the mystery has been solved. Your blood pressure is now coming down.

(2) Shows respect for the public. The public is savvy, possessing a certain "street-smartness" or skepticism born of the TV and Web age in which successes and failures are instantly brought into everyone's living room or desktop. More often than not, the public reacts positively to honest, clear communication. But they also hold companies accountable if they're not treated with respect and honesty. The public, when faced with news of difficult times for a company or brand—especially if employees or customers are affected—wants to hear that the company is concerned with the problem, has a commitment to finding the facts and fixing the problem, and is willing to explain what actions are being taken and what others are planned.

(3) Puts a human face on an otherwise anonymous corporation. This is especially important given the increasing anonymity of the Web and the "Press 1 if you know your party's extension" world. You may not know every detail of the crisis, but you are the senior face of the organization—and as we learned from the *Exxon Valdez* situation, there is a lot to be said about the presence of the CEO in times of extreme crisis. Your presence sends a clear message to employees, the community and the public, that you care and that you are accountable for the resolution of the crisis.

The delivery of an apology is one of the toughest moments in the life of a CEO, but there is evidence that beneficial effects of an apology can even be measured. Kellerman in her article cites: "In a recent British study of malpractice patients, 37% said they never would have gone to court in the first place had an explanation and an apology been extended." (Kellerman, "When Should a Leader Apologize and When Not?")

People will react differently to apologies. Some will accept, some will reject. In some cases, costly legal battles can be avoided. Retailer Eddie Bauer was caught in an embarrassing situation when one of their store security guards accused an African-American teenager of stealing a shirt when in reality the young man had purchased the shirt the day before. No apologies were offered. The family sued in what became a costly lawsuit. The teenager's father stated, "If they had apologized from the start or given some response, the lawsuit wouldn't happen. It feels like they don't care."

Consider some ways of expressing concern and an apology: "I understand how frustrating this must be." "I want to assure you of our deepest regret for this inconvenience. Now I would like to explain the steps we are taking to protect our customers."

And above all, keep it simple!

"Consumers are ready to forgive companies, but only if they think that an apology is sincere and is accompanied by corrective action," according to Gavin Fitzsimmons, associate professor of marketing at Duke University's Fuqua School of Business. *The Washington Post*, he points out, observed at the time that "what Johnson & Johnson executives have done is communicate the message that the company is candid, contrite and compassionate, committed to solving the murders and protecting the public." (Source: Robert J. Bliwise, "We Apologize: The Sorry State of Remorse," *Duke*, May-June, 2004)

Ask yourself the following questions when deciding on whether to issue an apology:

—Will I be protecting my own integrity?

—Is there ample evidence or sentiment among stakeholders that people are angry and have suffered some degree of harm?

—Will the apology accomplish anything? Will it, for example, calm some nerves, or serve as an introduction of a statement of what is happening?

—If I do not apologize, will anger and rumors increase?

Does a CEO need to have charisma?

Andy Gilman, who trained J&J chairman Jim Burke during the Tylenol tampering, and who has trained thousands of executives since, says that, "Very few people have charisma. Bill Clinton is clearly one—no matter your politics—who has it."

If you don't have the natural charisma, you can still create a better presence. It's lots of little things like handshakes, eye contact, clothing, smiling when you meet others, saying something positive about people you meet, expressing concern and curiosity.

When should the CEO speak?

Gilman also observed, "This was one of the most unique crises in that J&J did nothing wrong. In most other crises, there is—as the lawyers say—contributory negligence. While most companies don't deliberately do anything wrong, when a ship runs aground, that's the company fault. When the food is tainted, it's a company-caused accident. When the engineer falls asleep on the train that's a company problem. In this case, J&J didn't do anything wrong.

"J&J's famous Credo meant something," Gilman adds. "There was a value system in place. They also had good will deposits in their PR bank. They did make smart decisions. They pulled a strong team together and worked on it. They went above and beyond what they had to do. The government did not require tamper-proof packaging and at first not triplicate seals. And once they had answers and solutions they were very aggressive and proactive in their communications efforts."

Though press and employee statements acknowledging the situation should be issued quickly—generally within the first hour of a crisis—the decision on the availability of the CEO is a tougher one.

"'Putting a leader's face on crisis response is almost a necessity now, whether for potentially fatal product flaws or annoyances like flight delays,' said Sue Parenio, an associate professor of advertising at Boston University. 'Americans are so fed up with poor treatment from large corporate bureaucracies,' she said, 'that they will accept reassurance only from the top official.'" (Source: Julie Flaherty, "The Contrite CEO," *The New York Times*, September 3, 2000)

Some leaders rise to the occasion on the spot. While the concentration here is on the business side, not the government, it is all but impossible to ignore the calming leadership of Mayor Rudy Giuliani on 9/11 and in the days and months following the collapse of the World Trade Center. His ability to calm all of New York City and the surrounding area, to console the bereaved, and to encourage everyone to return to their normal lives—preventing the terrorists from saying they had won—will be part of history.

Some of the questions to ask to help make the decision on CEO availability as leading spokesperson:

—Where are the media? Does it look like there is national or international media interest?

—What is the extent of the crisis? Are there extensive injuries or fatalities?

—Has extensive harm been done either to a company site or the surrounding community?

—How long will it take to get to the crisis site?

—If I leave, am I confident in my deputy to carry on in the crisis room?

—Will I jump in too quickly before we know if this is a full-blown crisis? If I jump in too quickly, I could help elevate what is now an emergency into a full-blown crisis.

One aspect of management is predictable—the constant guessing, second-guessing and analyzing over what defines effective management, and a CEO in particular. Some of this includes fads and techniques. My favorite has always been "Management by Objective." This perfectly good, even wise phrase, was treated by many as a gee-whiz great idea. But, I asked, what's really new about the phrase? If you do not have an objective, what are you managing toward? The method, when in fashion, was nothing more than a series of obligatory charts and columns that consumed so much time there was scarcely any time left to actually manage.

Tom Peters, the "In Search of Excellence" guru, pushes quite rightly for nimble management, able and willing to turn and change as quickly as the market and the world dictate. Jack Welch, manager-turned-guru, reminds us that the best CEO is a coach, prodding, nurturing, guiding, encouraging, and praising managers.

But the time has come to add an important concept to the requirements of what makes an effective CEO: How does he act under the pressure of a crisis?

* * *

6   The Media—Big Pluses, Big Minuses

The media keep us connected and informed; they report the sensational, and they can be superficial.

The media play a central role in any company's crisis response. They are demanding; they are self-appointed investigators. They can be your effective messenger, or they can be your nagging enemy. Or both.

The media today are increasingly diverse and aggressive in their quest for bad news—and those companies that are able to protect their reputations and share price during a crisis are the ones that understand the media, understand the need to be open and responsive to the media, and are able to gain some control over the process.

The media today have greater speed and greater reach than ever, adding a whole new meaning to the phrase "mass media." *Mass* now means potentially reaching every person on Earth, either directly or indirectly, with the speed of light.

The media play a significant role in perpetuating (and sometimes creating) crises. The growth in mass communication has created intense competition among media outlets for swift headlines, which leads to occasional lapses in standards. While the media overwhelmingly provide responsible, urgent information to the public, they also continue to be cited for being too quick on occasion to rely on "sources," and often report on the latest scientific and opinion surveys without thoroughly vetting the sources or the information.

Today's media, more than ever, are incredibly diverse—from the in-depth, serious news coverage of the PBS NewsHour to the sensational, this-just-in scandal of the day reported by CNN's Nancy Grace. The rise of *USA Today*, Web sites, and the 24/7 cable news outlets have changed the face of news reporting, providing us with news when it happens and when we want it, and in small, easy-to-digest doses.

With the enormous panorama of competition for our eyes and ears, some of the media are on the decline, as they struggle to keep our attention and sell advertising.

NBC's *Today Show* hits the right buttons with an attractive mix of breaking news, celebrity interviews, wedding contests and the legal case of the moment. CNN and FoxNews bet on the sensational with a few prime-time exposé shows. Newspapers struggle and consolidate. All the while *USA Today* flourishes with news in smaller doses. The venerable *New York Times* maintains its mission of presenting "all the news that's fit to print" while trying some edgier coverage and features; and *The Wall Street Journal*, which finally carries photos, has lightened up with an array of personal features.

Local TV news remains as aggressive as ever. *The Ten O'Clock News* on the stations in Washington, D.C., and New York owned by Metromedia (now Fox), pioneered the "if it bleeds, it leads" strategy, and hundreds of other local TV news shows have followed suit with the daily rapes, murders or fires.

Howard Kurtz, *The Washington Post's* media correspondent described the changed landscape well:

"I like being able to click on newspapers from around the world, see bloggers smack each other around, Google any person or thing that pops into my brain, watch news videos (and some stupid stuff too) on YouTube, and generally surf till I drop." (Howard Kurtz, "Ink-Stained to Link-Stained: A Kvetch," *The Washington Post* December 25, 2006)

According to the Harris Poll (October 6, 2006), 33% of Americans report they have too much information in their lives to process all at one time.

Technology—all those small electronic devices—have changed our lives, too. In just the past few months I have conducted normal business with a little Blackberry—on the beach at 6 A.M., in the North Sea in the middle of the night, and sitting at my desk speaking with a client in Santiago as if he were next door. I routinely answer emails from London on the way to the Metro in the morning. And no one on the other end has any idea where I am.

Kurtz continues, "Now, liberated from the stronghold of CBS, NBC and ABC, we can watch news channels that match our political predilections, read Websites that reinforce our opinions, stream our favorite radio talkers through our computer speakers, download videos that mirror our obsessions, and select songs for our iPod playlists ... . [W]e can get anything we want, at the precise moment we want it, tailored to our merest whim." (Howard Kurtz, "Ink-Stained to Link-Stained: A Kvetch")

I thought I had a good chunk of my daily research under control when I signed on with CNN for news alerts. I was getting the news of the London terrorist arrests, presidential press conferences, even hurricane warnings. Then this popped up, as "breaking news," on my Blackberry:

"Whitney Houston is getting divorced."

And on another day, on the local alerts for danger—which I think means a nuclear attack or a hurricane—up popped the alert that two Rottweilers were on the loose in the Maryland suburbs.

But amid all the headlines today, business news has become a steady part of the news diet. Where business news was once considered dull and the job of the once-stuffy business papers, it is now mainstream news, helped along by the recent steady stream of scandals and by the realization that more Americans—including the average Joe and Jane—are shareholders in America's corporations, and they want to know what is going on.

Some of it even goes to extremes—as in the phenomenon of cable's Jim Kramer, a shouting, screaming reporter who chronicles the stock market news as if he were reporting the Super Bowl or a wrestling match.

Along comes your crisis, and the media are all over you—especially if the news is visual and has some real or suspected element of scandal. And everyone wants to be first with the news or the interview, including the newspapers, which no longer are dependent only on the delivery of the morning paper at the front door. They are updating their Web sites as the news pours in.

As Tim Wagner, American Airlines' Web master, reflecting on the events of 9/11, put it, "AMR's [parent company of American Airlines] crisis communications plan calls for 'communicating aggressively online because it is much more efficient than other media. If we can answer on the Web site the questions everyone asks, it frees our people to answer different questions over the telephone." (Tom Price, "Public Affairs Strategies in the Internet Age," The Foundation for Public Affairs, 2002)

With all these choices, consider some facts about how Americans— the Americans we want to understand our issues—are getting their news today.

For the TV viewers, Fox News is gaining steadily—with more than half of their viewers describing themselves as politically conservative, while CNN's audience leans more to the liberal. NPR, not surprisingly, also shows more liberal fans.

When news of a disaster strikes, the media are attracted like magnets and want instant answers, quotes from the biggest players they can get. And if the disaster satisfies their hunger for a story affecting people is also highly visual for TV and is easy to understand, they will not go away until the crisis ends. In the hunt for headlines and continuing coverage, they will look for the sensational and will play amateur detective, looking to fix blame. This simply is a fact of life—and one that will not change. It places a very special burden on the company in crisis to speak out quickly, truthfully and frequently. If you do not become part of the media mix in the first moments of your crisis, the media will find others to comment on your situation. You won't like it, and will take great pains to catch up.

For all news sources, there is a steady increase in international interest—no surprise, as terrorism and the war in Iraq are major concerns.

And the Web, which a few years ago was mostly the news source for younger people, is also attracting more interest from seniors and minorities. This is a natural evolution. The Web provides instant information and gratification. There it is, right in front of you when you want it.

Newspaper readership is the big divide. Six in ten people over 65 say they read a newspaper each day. Under 30? Only 23% report they read a paper. And across all demographics, newspapers are finding an increasing on-line readership. *The New York Times*, for example, attracts 1.5 million on-line readers each day, compared to 1.0 million for the paper edition.

And who among the public are the most knowledgeable when it comes to current affairs? Readers of *The New Yorker* and *The Atlantic*.

Well, you get the picture.

And this is an important picture, because we need to be aware, from an issue point of view, of how the grassroots—the voters, the supporters and opponents of your issues—are getting their news and information.

Except for newspapers, publications like *The New Yorker* and *The Atlantic*, and the *NewsHour* on PBS, most of the news is coming to U.S. in shorter chunks—the 2-minute story on the TV news; the quicker reads in *USA Today*; and headlines on the Web. Want more? Click on it. But not every headline earns a click.

What does all this mean for us—especially if we are trying to persuade the public to understand our point of view in a crisis?

The answer is: keep it simple, keep it short. This task is not as simple as it sounds—you need to avoid oversimplification while keeping it simple. As Mark Twain is reported to have said when admonished by an editor for the length of a manuscript: "If I'd had more time, it would have been shorter."

In the past year or so, the blog bandwagon has attracted huge interest. Is it justified? Well, maybe—and maybe not. According to Wikipedia.org, a blog (short for *Web log*) is "a Web page that serves as a publicly-accessible personal journal for an individual. Typically updated daily, blogs often reflect the personality of the author."

The definition of a blog is constantly evolving, though, as blogs move into the mainstream, shedding their image as the bastion of the self-obsessed who just have to self-express. Thousands of new blogs are being created every day, for all sorts of purposes. Rather than existing to catalog someone's personal life, many blogs serve as discussion communities about particular issues.

The blogs are still sorting themselves out. Some people blog for personal reasons, expressing themselves. Others have a deeper agenda to take on issues and causes. In the long run, blogging is here to stay, but it is not an all or nothing phenomenon. It is likely blogging will take many shapes and stay with us as another form of communication.

While companies are increasingly monitoring blogs and what they say about their companies and brands, the most prevalent use of blogs is in the political arena. We should not ignore them. Some analysis of this ultimate democratic communication tool will be useful

The talk-to-me blogs—these are the open dialogues—are an electronic community of people getting their own 15 seconds of Web fame, ranting to one another or networking and meeting new people in cyberspace. For some, it's like one big party.

These bloggers, the most prevalent, are posting their personal diaries or journals, and do not see their words as journalism. About half want to influence, the rest do it for personal satisfaction and expression. They write, in order of preference, about their life experiences, politics and government, and entertainment and sports.

They are young, with more than half under the age of 30. The rest are evenly fairly evenly divided but drop off considerably at age 65, where we find only 2% blogging. Not surprisingly, bloggers are heavy users of the Web, and 95% of bloggers report getting their news online. Asked why they get their news this way, many say it is simply more convenient. But they also report watching TV, listening to the radio and reading newspapers and magazines. These traditional media simply are not their dominant or sole source of news and information.

Most interesting, perhaps, is that more than half the bloggers do so under an assumed name. (Source: "A Portrait of the Internet's New Storytellers," *Pew Internet and American Life Project*, July 19, 2006)

Some blogs serve as ever-changing information sources. Take Wikipedia—a kind of encyclopedia Britannica of the Web, where anyone can enter a change. Well, folks, not everyone is a qualified or credible source. So what we have is one huge unreliable source with some good stuff and some not-so-good stuff.

The industry or company blogs are next, and they are worth watching, for they may contain some early warnings of problems. Monitoring these is a big job, but technology will make it easier.

And finally, we have the consumer blogs. You can go online and check what people are saying about a restaurant, a hotel, a product. Travel Advisor.com, for example, can make or break a hotel. On the consumer product side, online shopping has become easier. Confronted with choosing among two dozen digital recorders on Amazon.com, I easily chose the one I did because a previous customer had said, "even my mother can figure this one out."

According to a Pew Research Center survey, only 27% of Internet users in America bother to read blogs. (Stephen Baker and Heather Green, "Blogs Will Change Your Business," *Business Week Online*, May 2, 2005)

According to another survey—The Makovsky 2006 Survey of Corporate Blogging—only 5% of Fortune 1000 executives were convinced to a great extent that corporate blogging is growing in credibility. (Press release, "Fortune 1000 Senior Executives Slow to React to the Growing Credibility of Corporate Blogs, New Survey Concludes," Makovsky and Company, May 3, 2006)

In yet another study— this one by Hill & Knowlton—we find that only 17% of Wall Street analysts see blogging as fairly important, compared to 71% for articles in the business media and 85% for the company website. ("Hill & Knowlton's Corporate Reputation Watch," May 31, 2006)

If you're tempted to start a company blog, remember:

–Have a good reason. Answering angry customers could be a reason–but remember that what you say and how you say it reflects on the entire company.

–Keep it simple and easy to navigate.

–This is all permanent stuff. Once you've done it, it does not go away.

Pete Snyder, President of New Media Strategies and one of the pioneers in advising companies on the blog phenomenon, put it this way:

"The worst possible thing for a company to do in the face of constant criticism is to take the imperial ivory tower 'we don't respond' tack, otherwise known as the 'head in sand' ostrich strategy, which allows critics to control the conversation and amplify what should have been a teapot tempest into a full-blown riot. If the basis for attacks on a company is false, it is critical to address them in forums, via company blogs, and social media.

Consumers don't read press releases, and it is critical to get the other side of a story to them in the same format that they are encountering negative news. When presented with the facts in a plain-spoken, straightforward manner, online communities usually squash untrue rumors at an astonishing speed.

"If however, the accusations that are being leveled against a firm are, at the end of the day valid, a different communication strategy is needed. First, acknowledging the problem is key—customers appreciate honesty and the recognition that they've been heard. Second is presenting a plan on how it will be addressed, or if it can't be resolved, an open and honest explanation of why not. Lastly, providing updates on a regular basis lets the public know that the issue hasn't fallen off the radar screen." (Source: Interview with author)

The media trend these days is to do instant polling on CNN, NBC's *Today Show*, and others. "Go online and tell U.S. what you think of this or that." Is this valid? I think not—those who cast the votes are self-selecting based on their inclination to cast a vote, whether they have the time do so, etc. Be wary of these polls. They may be fun, but they are not valid samples.

Apart from the gathering of information on an issue you already know exists, what is the value of monitoring the media? It has enormous value in issue detection and preventing an issue from becoming a crisis. Consider, for example, all the information you can gather from news coverage and reports of how another company or industry has faced an issue. And with this information, ask yourself the tough questions. Could this happen here? If it did could we handle it, and how? Are we vulnerable too? And if we are, what can we do about this early warning right now?

The Tylenol tamperings proved that the media can create an instant hero, as they did with Jim Burke, J&J's chairman. Did the media deserve all the credit? No. Burke was perfect. These were unsolved murders. The product was very popular, and Burke was Mr. Sincere and Mr. Caring—the uncle next door. The alternative is to create an instant symbol of the uncaring corporation, as in the case of Lawrence Rawl, Exxon's CEO, who avoided the media at the expense of the corporation's reputation.

Part II

CLOSING THE READINESS GAP

7   A Prescription for 100% Protection and Readiness

"The only thing harder than planning for an emergency is explaining why you didn't."

—Anonymous

As noted earlier (see p. 6), 75% of American businesses have a crisis plan. This leaves a "readiness gap" of at least 25% in our nation's private sector crisis preparedness. Until there is clear accountability and in some cases financial incentives—whether driven by boards who demand crisis planning as part of CEO salary and bonus, insurance premium incentives, or tax breaks—we will continue to have a checkerboard of companies in varying states of readiness. Only the visionaries and the vulnerables who have been through the worst of the worst disasters will have the guts to be ready.

The real truth—what should be the best incentive for preparation—also lies in the all-important share price for publicly traded companies. There is frequently a correlation between high-profile crises and a decline in share price. And many companies—the unprepared—never recover.

The sad truth is that our collective level of denial is way too high for today's high-risk world. Will it change? What will it take for the avoiders—those who push preparation to the back edges of the budget—to join the ranks of the visionaries and the veterans of tough times?

After 25 years of development, the specialty of crisis management is ripe to become a profession. This will come about through the creation of a professional organization—for the sake of discussion, let's call this yet-to-be-created organization the International Crisis Management Institute—and an accelerated effort to force crisis management to become a corporate governance issue. This will not be an easy task, but the time has come to begin. It first will require leadership—from government, the law, companies, and the crisis management profession.

Despite thousands of how-to efforts—not least of which is the Department of Homeland Security's ready.gov—there are no pressures and incentives to close the 25% gap. If crisis readiness among American business continues to improve at roughly 2% a year, we may easily be looking at another dozen plus years before we are 100% crisis-ready. That rate of improvement is unacceptable.

The odds of accelerating this readiness are low unless new bold steps are taken to keep the momentum going at those companies that are prepared, and to propel those who do little or nothing. It's going to take accountability and it's going to take a professional approach to standards and training.

Moving to the 100% level will require:

—Accelerated efforts to convince board members that crisis readiness is a corporate governance issue

—The creation of an international standards and training institute

—Shareholder efforts to hold corporations accountable for crisis planning

First Steps

A number of efforts are underway to create generally accepted standards, through the International Standards Organization and others. One of the most ambitious efforts to create national standards for crisis readiness and response has been the work by the National Fire Protection Association. The standards document, called NFPA 1600, is, according to NFPA, a "Standard on Disaster/Emergency Management and Business Continuity Programs," and it may become the industry standard for all organizations, including governments and businesses. If you are in the business of providing emergency, disaster, or business-continuity planning or services, you had better get to know "1600" soon.

The standard was endorsed by the 9/11 Commission and is now endorsed, but not mandated, in pending Congressional legislation called "Improving America's Security Act of 2007." In the summary of provisions for the legislation, Title VII states:

"In order to promote private sector preparedness, this title establishes a voluntary certification program to assess whether a private sector entity complies with voluntary preparedness standards. Working with organizations such as the American National Standards Institute (ANSI)

and the private sector advisory councils created by the Homeland Security Act of 2002, the Secretary would develop the preparedness standards and implement the program, which would be managed by ANSI and other similarly qualified entities. Under the program, companies wishing to be certified as prepared would have their applications reviewed by third parties accredited by organizations such as ANSI to determine whether the companies comply with the standards. The title also requires the FEMA regional offices to coordinate with the private sector to ensure private sector preparedness. "

This encyclopedic document has been reviewed by countless experts, and the result is quite thorough. It can be a useful document or checklist for middle managers. By itself, however, it is not a panacea, for several reasons.

This is a very dense, detailed document. This is a very dense, detailed document. It does not by any means appear to be a document that is designed to attract the attention of directors or CEOs. Unlike the efforts by the Business Roundtable to advise CEOs on their role in crisis management, the NFPA 1600 standard-setting does not emphasize the CEO or the organizational challenges of leadership.. Unlike the efforts by the Business Roundtable to advise CEOs on their role in crisis management, the NFPA 1600 standard-setting does not emphasize the CEO or the organizational challenges of leadership.

As Joseph D. Whitley, the former General Counsel to the Department of Homeland Security, put it: "NFPA 1600 is an important first step. However, it is only a first step: NFPA 1600 is a generic document that provides guidance at 30,000 feet. Moving closer to 100% preparedness will require organizations to implement the general features of NFPA 1600, but to drill down much deeper. Tying this to incentives to encourage such positive behavior is a useful approach. Nonetheless, we have also seen an upsurge in preparedness that is the result of regulation. Most recently, Congress has required the Department of Homeland Security to create national standards to enhance security at the nation's most at-risk chemical facilities." (Source: Interview with author)

The idea of Congressional "voluntary" endorsement, which would have no force of law, does little to advance the standards. American companies face huge regulatory and compliance burdens already. Any new federal burden, even a voluntary one, is likely to send shivers down corporate spines.

And finally, given the growing distaste for bureaucracy, the NFPA 1600—which looks like, feels like and reads like a government manual— needs to be made user-friendly if it is to succeed at all.

This document or similar efforts could be part of the proposed International Crisis Management Institute discussed in this chapter. By itself, however, it is another bureaucratic standard.

Crisis Readiness Is a Governance Issue

We've now entered a wakeup call period, where boards are looking around and saying 'it could happen to us.' In fact, it is astonishing to me to see the movement among board members regarding crisis management."

—Suzanne Hopgood
Interview with the author

As recently as 2004, when Harris Interactive polled executives on whether risk management was a board-level issue, only 65% of U.S. boards saw risk management as an issue. In contrast, 93 % of European companies regard risk as a board-level issue. This is essentially due to legislation requiring companies to disclose their risk management activities. (Source: "Managing Business Risks," Harris Interactive, June, 2004)

"Effective crisis management, including planning for and responding to crisis, depends on an honest and courageous chief executive who is willing to meet challenges head-on, and a board that is willing to ask questions, take action, and even take charge when needed. Even more fundamentally, a corporation's response to risk and potential crisis depends on a strong foundation of corporate governance." (Report of the NACD Blue Ribbon Commission on Risk Oversight)

"[E]nsuring that sound crisis response planning is done by management is one of the essential functions of the board. The board's oversight responsibility is generally well understood in areas such as strategy, budgeting, capital transactions, acquisitions and CEO succession. It is equally the board's responsibility to see that crisis response planning receives the appropriate emphasis among the many issues competing for the attention of the board and management. There is a broad range of possible action by a company in the area of crisis response planning—the board's judgment on how much is appropriate should be expressly brought to bear on this question. It is too important to leave to management without board oversight." (Suzanne Hopgood and Michael Tankersely, "Is My Company Really Ready for a Crisis?" *Corporate Board Member*, April 12, 2006)

A revolution in the role of the board of directors is underway. Sarbanes-Oxley, recent corporate scandals and shareholder pressure are tearing down the walls around the traditional board room.

"Now the heat on directors is growing more intense. Their reputations are increasingly at risk when the companies they watch over are tainted by scandal. Their judgment is being questioned by activist shareholders outraged by sky-high pay packages. And investors and regulators are subjecting their actions to higher scrutiny. Long gone are the days when a director could get away with a quick rubber-stamp of a CEO's plans.

"The old rules of civility that discouraged directors from asking managers tough or embarrassing questions are eroding. At the same time, board members are being forced to devote more time and energy to many of their most important duties: setting CEO compensation, overseeing the auditing of financial statements, and, when needed, investigating crises. That's the good news. The bad news is they are so busy delving into the minutiae of compliance that they don't have nearly as much time to advise corporate chieftains on strategy.

"The increased scrutiny on boards means that a perfunctory review will not suffice if a scandal strikes. Directors can no longer afford to defer to management in a crisis. They must roll up their sleeves and move into watchdog mode." (Nanette Byrnes and Jane Sasseen, "Board of Hard Knocks," *Business Week*, January 22, 2007)

"More board members are independent. More are meeting on their own without management. Directors can be seen mingling with employees to get the inside scoop on emerging or festering problems. A surprising 46% of boards now require that directors visit company operations." (Source: "Mercer Delta Corporate Board Survey Results," USC/ Marshall School of Business, March, 2005)

The National Association of Corporate Directors' Blue Ribbon Commission on Risk Oversight states that "if true reform is to occur, directors must be a permanent and active part of the solution. Above all, the Commission continues, "risk oversight must be a priority for all boards, especially in turbulent times."

Oversight, according to the NACD, refers to the exercise of the director's fiduciary duty of care on behalf of the owners, and by extension, other stakeholders in the corporation. Under normal circumstances, boards have a primary fiduciary duty to shareholders. Indeed, so-called "agency theory," a frequent topic in the academic literature on corporate governance, says that managers are merely the agents of stockholders, whose money they are handling. And that directors are there to make sure that manager-agents act properly. (Report of the NACD Blue Ribbon Commission on Risk Oversight, 2002, 2003, 2006)

Suzanne Hopgood and Michael Tankersely (also authors of **Board Leadership for the Company in Crisis**, National Association of Corporate Directors, 2005), raise the direct question: "Who is responsible for assuring that a company is well prepared to meet the crises of 2006 and beyond?"

Their answer: "The board. This is not to say that management's role is not critical to an effective crisis planning and response process, or that the CEO should not be taking the lead. The primary task of a company's leaders, according to Peter Drucker, is 'to make sure of the institution's capacity for survival–to make sure of its structural strength and soundness, of its capacity to survive a blow, and to adapt to sudden change.' It is much too important," they emphasize, "to leave to management without board oversight." (Hopgood and Tankersely, "Is My Company Really Ready for a Crisis?")

Hopgood and Tankersley point to "six compelling reasons why directors should insist that management and board attention be focused on crisis response planning:

Even limited planning will help the company to avoid common blunders, particularly in managing communications, that turn manageable crises into disasters.

Planning will decrease the number of decisions that must be made in the early stages of a crisis and allow more attention to those that remain, improving the quality of decision making.

Organizing the company's crisis response team in advance will allow the necessary expertise to be assembled quickly and begin working immediately when a crisis hits. Good outside advisors are not easy to find; planning will help assure they are available when needed.

Many crises begin as manageable problems that then escalate to disastrous proportion. Focused crisis planning makes it more likely that potential crises will be contained before they escalate.

Directors are obligated to use ordinary care in their decision making and oversight of the company. Ordinarily careful and prudent individuals buy insurance and make plans to weather personal disasters. Companies should engage in crisis response planning for the same reasons.

While the prospect of directors encountering personal liability for failing to engage in crisis planning is generally remote, when a crisis does arrive, ill-advised responses of the board, management, and employees can create liability for individuals and the organization. Crisis planning will identify these risks and how to avoid them."

The addition of a board level Crisis Preparedness Committee, charged with overseeing their company's crisis preparedness, will require several steps:

–Basic understanding of risk management and risk communication.
–Benchmarking or guidance to determine what an effective plan is. A number of benchmarks exist, including *The Business Roundtable's Post-9/11 Crisis Communications Tool Kit*; and the NFPA 1600 guidance.
–Incentives that can be tied directly to CEO compensation. It seems mundane but simple: Hold CEOs accountable for the clarity and completeness of their plans, scheduling for training and simulations, etc. These are easily documented accomplishments, and their importance is of such vital nature that a CEO who avoids these obligations should be penalized where it hurts—in his checkbook.
–Continued awareness and briefings for new directors, such as those the NACD now conducts for hundreds of new directors, which are a major step toward creating accountability

Specifically, boards can begin the accountability process by implementing the following steps:

–Demanding to see the existing crisis plans
–Authorizing budget expenditures for crisis planning
–Asking tough questions, such as: Where is all this cash coming from? Where did the company's cash go?
–Determining if there are any lapses in ethics.
–Ensuring the company has identified in the most direct way (i.e., without probability weighting) all possible crises. And if any of these were to occur, that the company is ready to respond. And if not, why? And what will it take to be ready?
–Being ready to step in quickly in the worst-case situation where senior management may be implicated in a crisis and not be able to function

As Jack and Suzy Welch put it: "[T]he board must assess and challenge management. It must get out of headquarters to see if employees in the field are really carrying out the mission and hewing it to the values that the brass espouses in the boardroom. But ultimately, a board and management must play on the same team, not operate at cross-purposes." (Jack and Suzy Welch, "Ideas The Welch Way," *Business Week*, December 25. 2006/ January 1, 2007)

Boards will need credible, generally accepted guidelines

The National Association of Corporate Directors' *Board Leadership for the Company in Crisis* and The Business Roundtable's *Post-9/11 Crisis Communication Tool Kit* are important resources for board members. Books and Web sites are filled with ideas for the ground rules for crisis planning. The problem is that no one set of ideas has risen to the surface as the generally accepted guideline for best practice.

Shareholder Activism Is Coming of Age

I recall having the outspoken Evelyn Y. Davis on my Washington TV program in the 1970s. Davis, who owned one share of stock in lots of Fortune 500s, made a career of being the annoying but often correct gadfly at annual meetings. She was outspoken but essentially alone. While she attracted lots attention from the media, she made few inroads because she had no constituency or support.

Then came Ralph Nader and unions, religious organizations and others, who bought a few shares, giving them the platform for urging environmental and social changes.

Over the past several years, shareholder activism has risen to a more sophisticated art, with major funds attracting attention with resolutions on a variety of issues. Make no mistake—the activists have the resources to mount campaigns, use the media, create blogs and create support. 2006 and 2007 were watershed years for shareholder activism. First came the ouster, after shareholder pressure, of the chief executives at Pfizer and Sovereign Bank. Then Ralph V. Whitworth—who had helped found the United Shareholders Association in 1986, and had selected about 50 companies a year to be the subject of embarrassing questions—applied the final pressure to unseat The Home Depot's chairman, Robert Nardelli, for his large compensation package and deteriorating share price. Whitworth, whose fund owns a 1.2% stake in The Home Depot, may yet win a board seat as well. And, observers say, The Home Depot is but the beginning.

"Activist shareholders have a power and audience beyond what they've ever enjoyed," said Howard Steinberg, a lawyer who advises corporate boards and deal makers. "They're developing a credible track record, and as a result, more and more managers are forced to engage with them. Activists' time has come."(Source: Charles Duhigg, "Disgruntled Investors Get Spot in Center Ring," *The San Diego Union-Tribune*, January 5, 2007)

While compensation is the primary concern of shareholder activists, and it is gaining steam rapidly, it is reasonable to expect that another topic on their list can and should be crisis readiness. This is a logical step, because there is clear evidence that a poorly handled crisis, especially by a company with a stale plan or no plan at all, risks reputational disaster—with a resulting decline in share price.

Shareholder pressure may not always be played out in the headlines, but it is there. As John Wilcox, head of corporate governance at the giant TIAA-Cref fund said, "Our strategy in the activist area is to meet one-on-one with managements. Quiet diplomacy is the way we work."(Source: Jeff Nash, "The Payparazzi," *Financial Week*, January 15, 2007)

While pressure mounts from the new activists, the traditional boycott is still alive. Boycotts are part of our history. Though their results have been uneven, they are with us and should not be ignored. While the vast number of boycotts are annoyances and embarrassments to companies, with little affect on sales, some have made deep and lasting inroads.

The most successful boycott in American history was the Boston Tea Party in 1773, staged to rebel against taxation without representation. The Montgomery Bus Boycott of 1955, after Rosa Parks was arrested for refusing to move to the back of the bus, was a success for civil rights

Several years ago, People for the Ethical Treatment of Animals waged an unrelenting, often invasive campaign against the killing of animals for fur coats. Countless consumers quickly stopped wearing their fur coats in public, for fear they would be splashed with paint by the PETA pickets. And many more stopped buying fur coats, forcing the closing of many shops. Several years later, the industry has slowly rebounded. But some retailers are gone forever. Though less violent, PETA's boycott campaign against the cosmetic companies forced the end of most animal testing.

Today's boycotters have far more tools available to them than the citizens of 1773 Boston did. The Web has had an enormous impact, giving activists the means, for little or no cost, to share information, ideas and plans, and to speak out on blogs and other sites.

Other boycotts go on for years and never seem to go away. One such boycott is the movement to ban so-called bio-engineered or "frankenfoods." I was a consultant for two of the annual scientific meetings of the Biotechnology Industry Organization's. With more than 10,000 scientists coming together for several days, there was concern about the effects of protesters outside the convention halls. While they were not able to block entrance to the halls, as they intended, they did attract a great deal of media attention because of their colorful parades and loud protest statements. They still are a force, perhaps in large part because they are objecting to many food products that have not yet materialized.

Other boycotts are desperate efforts for well-intentioned causes, that simply go nowhere. But they all stir corporate anxiety. Several years ago, when the French were testing nuclear weapons on remote Pacific islands, protesters threatened French consumer products companies with boycotts if they did not lobby the government to stop the testing. The strategy did not work. The companies did not want to become involved in the issue, and the actual boycotts faded quickly. And the boycott of Exxon gas stations in protest against the **Exxon Valdez** crisis, lingered for years, while Exxon's profits soared.

Whether you are faced with a boycott, with pickets and blogs, or shareholder pressure, the strategy for the company should be the same: Find out as much as you can about the protesters and their claims. Meet with them. During these discussions, determine the legitimacy of the issue and what it might take to come to terms. In most cases it will be a long process, but it must begin.

The International Crisis Management Institute: The Time Has Come

There is an urgent need for the establishment of crisis management standards, housed within a new organization created for the specific purpose of creating these standards and a number of other steps to assist companies in their crisis planning and response. Without these standards, board members will be handicapped, unable to ask all the right questions and to measure their companies' readiness.

The ICMI will:

—Set clear, senior-level crisis management standards for directors, CEOs and their senior staffs.
—Certify member company crisis mangers after completion of ICMI training
—Conduct programs in crisis management
   Note: It is not the intention of ICMI to certify individual company crisis readiness programs, for to do so raises certain legal and confidentiality issues that are not appropriate for a professional organization to engage in. However, ICMI will regularly provide self-assessment tools for member companies to use in their regular reviews of readiness.

—Keep members abreast of developments and best practices in crisis management

—Provide reference and referral information in response to member requests

—Provide specific consultations as may be requested by members before, during and after a crisis

—Offer guidance in understanding the complex government disaster plans

A Rationale for the Creation of the International Crisis Management Institute

As the crisis communication and management discipline is so new, there has been no effort to bring it to the next level—i.e., to create standards, to train and certify corporate crisis managers in a unified way, to provide a library of cases and news coverage, to act as a clearinghouse for the resources a company would need in a crisis, etc.

Nonetheless, it is interesting to note the related efforts that have developed since 9/11—a foreshadowing of the ICMI effort. These related efforts include:

—U.S.-based university efforts to establish in-house institutes or courses in crisis management. George Washington University has established an Institute for Crisis, Disaster and Risk Management, based on courses which require attendance throughout an academic year. New York University has established the Center for Catastrophic Preparedness and Response. This appears to be a major imitative, with initial funding of $7 million, to be used for a variety of activities, including research, program development, and training.

—The University of Hong Kong offers the Executive Certificate in Strategic Crisis Management. It is based on a 30-hour course (presumably over a semester) that teaches the basics of crisis management.

—A number of courses are being offered in security by the American Society for International Security and the Disaster Recovery Institute, and in business continuity and recovery by the *Disaster Recovery Journal*.

While these efforts are indications that the crisis management and communication specialty is being taken to the next level, they fall short of the mark because each represents only a small part of the big picture.

The time has come to take the crisis management discipline to the next level and to provide, in one place, the resources that companies need to be better prepared. By doing so in a clear, affordable and credible structure, it can greatly help businesses protect their resources.

After decades of crisis experience by American businesses, a solid body of crisis information, examples and assistance exists—but there is little linkage among government, business and academic communities. And there is no single source to provide information, resources, and senior counsel for situations that threaten the well-being, reputations, and day-to-day operations of organizations.

ICMI would be a professional resource for public and private sector organizations worldwide—at any stage, whether in the middle of a crisis or at the early stage of planning—looking for help. ICMI would be the generally recognized crisis certification and standard-setting body,

A Blueprint for the ICMI

Following is a suggested charter statement for the ICMI:

The International Crisis Management Institute (hereafter referred to as the ICMI is an international non-profit membership organization. The ICMI's purpose is to serve as the principal coordinating body for the setting of standards for private-sector crisis readiness, response and recovery. In cases where specialized standard-setting exists (e.g., the Business Continuity Institute or NFP 1600), the ICMI will embrace and recognize those organizations as independent, established entities. In areas where standards do not exist or where, in the judgment of the ICMI board of trustees, existing standards should be expanded and made more workable, the ICMI will undertake such standards-settings as ICMI responsibilities.

The ICMI will be governed by a board of trustees comprised of no more than 20 experienced professionals drawn from the senior ranks of business, consulting, government, and trade and professional organizations. A maximum of four additional non-voting seats on the board will represent senior government departments involved in crisis readiness and response. The chair of the board of trustees will be chosen by majority vote from among the board members and will serve a two-year term.

The board will have final authority for such matters as strategic direction, budget approval, and the hiring of the ICMI Executive Director. The board will also ensure that ICMI sets an example by having in place its own state-of-the-art-crisis response plan.

The ICMI executive director will be the organization's chief operating officer and will be responsible for the design and implementation of all programs as well as the administration of the organization.

The ICMI is a membership organization and will derive its operating budget from the fees paid by members. Members will be companies, both public and private, of any size and headquartered in locations throughout the world. Additional funds may from time to time be derived from charitable foundations and may be for general or special project purposes (e.g., for a special study in crisis management). The ICMI membership fee structure is intended to be as simple as possible but mindful of the budget parameters of all companies.

Members who partake in specific training programs or who wish to purchase specific publications will be billed for them in addition to their annual membership fees.

Government agencies and non-profit organizations engaged in whole or in part in the field of crisis management will be eligible for membership at no cost.

Model Training Program

Day 1:
Crisis Communications Overview
    a. Definitions
    b. Crisis v. Emergency
    c. Reputation Management
    d. Role of the communicator
Discussion of 10 Most Important Crises and Lessons Learned
Crisis Communications as a Part of Public Relations
Crisis Communications and its Links to Other Disciplines
    a. IT
    b. Law enforcement
    c. Public safety
    d. Investor relations
    e. Organization security

Day 2:
Creating a Crisis Plan
    a. Who should be on the team
    b. Assessing vulnerabilities
    c. Interacting with other crisis planning
    d. What goes into a Crisis War Room
    e. Utilizing the Web

Day 3:
Testing Skills
    Table top exercise
    Training and response

Summary and Next Steps

PART III

THE TOOL KIT

8   Tools You Can Use

A Guide to Commonly Used Terms

The crises of the past few years and the creation of the Department of Homeland Security have spawned a new vocabulary, with acronyms and shorthand. Following is a guide to some of the more commonly used terms.

Blogs
According to Wikipedia.org, a blog (short for *Web log*) is "a Web page that serves as a publicly-accessible personal journal for an individual. Typically updated daily, blogs often reflect the personality of the author".

The definition of blog is constantly evolving, though, as blogs move into the mainstream, shedding their image as the bastion of the self-obsessed who just have to self-express. Thousands of new blogs are being created every day, for all sorts of purposes. Rather than existing only to catalog someone's personal life, many blogs serve as discussion communities about particular issues.

Bridging
The interview technique that calls for the person answering a question to, after answering the question, hold the moment and emphasize a different—though related—point by using such bridging phrases as, "But the important point to note is...," or "Let me also point out that..."

Business Continuity
The processes and procedures an organization puts in place to assure that essential functions can continue during and after a disaster.

Call Tree

A structured process that allows members of the crisis team to be contacted rapidly—either by a series of personal calls or by an automated system.

CEO COMLINK^{SM}

A tool through which CEOs can communicate directly with the Department of Homeland Security in the event of a national crisis. CEOs must register and be credentialed before they can gain access to this crisis tool and receive separate instructions on using the system. The program is coordinated by the Business Roundtable.

Dirty Bomb

A crude method for spreading radiation over a substantial area. Note: A dirty bomb does not create a nuclear blast. It is made by packing dynamite or other conventional explosive with any type of radioactive material—e.g., isotopes used in x-ray machines—and, when detonated, it spreads the radioactive material.

GETS Cards

Government Emergency Telecommunications Service (GETS) cards, which provide priority telephone connectivity during an emergency to parties considered by the federal government to have a role in addressing issues related to homeland security

Incident Commander

A government official in charge of coordinating resources and strategies in the event of an emergency.

Incident of National Significance (INS)

An actual or potential high-impact event that requires immediate and extensive coordination of federal government resources to save lives and minimize damage.

International Standards Organization (ISO)

A network of the national standards institutes of 157 countries, on the basis of one member per country, with a Central Secretariat in Geneva, Switzerland, that coordinates the system. ISO is a non-governmental organization; its members are not, as in the case of the United Nations, delegations of national governments. Nevertheless, ISO occupies a special position between the public and private sectors. Many of its member institutes are part of the governmental structure of their countries, or are mandated by their government. Other members have their roots uniquely in the private sector, having been set up by national partnerships of industry associations. Therefore, ISO is able to act as a bridging organization in which a consensus can be reached on solutions that meet both the requirements of business and the broader needs of society, such as the needs of stakeholder groups like consumers and users.

Interoperability
The ability of first-response agencies (fire, police, emergency medical services) to communicate with each other during an emergency or disaster.

ISACs
Information Sharing and Analysis Centers, which are associated with each of the major economic sectors, including communications, electricity, finance, transportation, information technology, public transit, and water. The ISACs provide a framework for sharing physical- and cyber-security information.

Joint Field Office (JFO)
A temporary federal facility established locally to provide a central point for federal, state and local executives with responsibility for incident direction and operations.

National Incident Management System (NIMS)
A Department of Homeland Security plan developed so that responders from different jurisdictions and disciplines can work together to deal with natural disasters and emergencies, including acts of terrorism. The plan includes a unified approach to incident management, standard command and management structures, and emphasis on preparedness, mutual aid and resource management. The NIMS Integration Center (NIC) oversees all aspects of NIMS including the development of compliance criteria and implementation activities at federal, state and local levels. It provides guidance and support to jurisdictions and incident management and responder organizations as they adopt the system.

National Infrastructure Protection Plan (NIPP)
A Department of Homeland Security plan that provides a coordinated approach to critical infrastructure and key resource protection roles and responsibilities for federal, state, local, tribal, and private sector

security partners. The NIPP sets national priorities, goals, and requirements for effective distribution of funding and resources that will help ensure that the government, economy, and public services continue in the event of a terrorist attack or other disaster.

National Response Plan (NRP)
The National Response Plan, which establishes a comprehensive, all-hazards approach to managing domestic incidents. The plan forms the basis of how the federal government coordinates with state, local, and tribal governments, and with the private sector, during incidents.

NFPA 1600
A detailed checklist of suggested crisis planning requirements, created for the American National Standards Institute by the National Fire Protection Association.

Patriot Act
Acronym for the U.S. law: Provide Appropriate Tools Required to Intercept and Obstruct Terrorism.

Ready.gov
A national Department of Homeland Security public service campaign designed to educate Americans to prepare for and respond to emergencies, including natural disasters and threat of terrorist attacks. The series includes components for the home, children and business.

Risk communication
A specialized area of communication that is based on well-researched guidelines for communicating risk information to the public.

Shelter in Place
Staying in the building you are in, if it is habitable, in the event of an emergency involving air contamination.

Terrorist Threat Integration Center (TTIC)
A unit of the Department of Homeland Security responsible for gathering and analyzing threat information from across the entire federal government. The TTIC is based at the Central Intelligence Agency (CIA).

TOPOFF

Part of the national terrorism response exercise program, TOPOFF is a congressionally mandated exercise program designed to test and strengthen local, state and federal government resources.

9   A Standard Approach to Crisis Planning

This chapter presents a standard approach to crisis planning for board members and senior management, based on collective experiences and best practices. While there is no one-size-fits-all approach, there is some common ground that all can use as a foundation.

The Top Things You Need to Do to Be Crisis-Ready

–Conduct an annual checkup to see where you fit on the readiness scale.
–Have a plan, and keep it simple and up-to-date.
–Make crisis preparation a full-time commitment.
–Think prevention.
–Have a backup for everything—from people to infrastructure.
–Remember your employees and their families.
–Keep your suppliers and customers aware of your plans.
–Be ready to explain risks to the public in a sensitive, open manner.
–Practice according to a schedule—and stick to it.
–Don't hide—don't even consider it.
–And remember the basics:
  Have crisis and security executives report directly to the CEO.
  Keep the plan simple, and
  Practice, Practice, Practice

Helping the Board Get Started

The first and most important step for any company is the creation of the permanent Crisis Governance Committee of the board. This concept should become standard for all companies, assuring that crisis readiness is a required, standard operating procedure.

This will not happen overnight, but the time has come to begin. And the first step is the creation of a Crisis Governance Committee.

The Crisis Governance Committee of the board should have specific oversight over the company's crisis preparedness plans and monitor the plan's status, relevance and utility. Should a crisis occur, the Governance Committee would be available for counsel, but not involved in the day-to-day and hour-by-hour management of the crisis. However, should the CEO or other senior officers of the company be unavailable or otherwise not appropriate for involvement in the crisis response, the board should immediately step in to assume management of the crisis. A final step, and an equally important one, is the board's review of the lessons learned from any drill or actual crisis, with assurance that steps will be taken for continuous improvement based on those lessons learned.

Once a Crisis Governance Committee has been formed, the first step for the Committee should be a review of the company's crisis procedures. The score-based tool presented below is offered as a means for reviewing the company's crisis plan.

The Plan

In the months following the Tylenol tamperings, as we worked to define the parameters for crisis preparedness, the trend was toward creation of large manuals. These gradually gave way to shorter, user-friendly manuals of less than 40 pages. They were still too long to be useful during a crisis, though they had an important place during training. The state of the art today includes the crisis manual—preferably called the Crisis Resource Manual—and a pocket card that lists key contact information and checklists reminding the team members of their duties.

Crisis Plan Diagnosis

We are a nation of scorekeepers. We have scores for football, cholesterol, and IQs. The time has come for a crisis readiness score that can graphically highlight a company's readiness. Companies of all sizes and in all industries face common crisis readiness challenges. The following tool will help appraise any company's readiness:

Score each item on a scale of 1 to 3, with 3 being the best. Looking at the score for each item and for the total will give you a clear—perhaps startling —picture of where the company stands.

The scale is based on the following:

1 =   Unacceptable

2 =   Marginal, still needs improvement

3: =   Acceptable

Score

1. Does a crisis plan exist?

2. Is there a pocket card version of the plan?

3. Has the plan been updated in the past three months?

4. Is there a dedicated situation room?

5. Can an existing conference room quickly be converted into a situation room?

6. Is the CEO directly involved in crisis planning?

7. Has the CEO been briefed on the company's crisis plan within the past 30 days?

8. Is the CEO the chair of the crisis team?

9. Is the crisis team membership clearly defined?

10. Is the responsibility for crisis readiness a full-time staff function?

11. Has the company identified all potential risks without regard for their probability?

12. Has the following been asked regarding each risk:
A. If this happened today, how well equipped would we be to handle it?
B. Has everything reasonable been done to reduce or eliminate this risk?

13. If a crisis occurred in the company today, could the crisis team come together within 30 minutes?

14. If the primary team members are not available, are designated backups available?

15. Can the plan pass a Contact Test? Specifically, assuming the plan contains contact information for the crisis team and you placed calls to six team members on their home or cell phones, would you reach them after hours?

16. Is there a procedure for regularly verifying contact information?

17. Do your HQ and branch operations know all there is to know about local emergency resources—governmental and non-governmental?

18. Are crisis simulations conducted at least semiannually

19. Once these simulations have been scheduled, are they considered firm commitments? Or are they postponed frequently?

20. Is there a protocol for follow-through on the lessons learned and changes that should be made to the plan?

21. Are newly appointed members of the crisis team trained to understand their responsibilities?

22. Is there a regular schedule for evacuation drills?

23. Are the evacuation drills successively challenging? Or are they the same old, "go to the nearest exit, descend the stairs, and wait until the all-clear is sounded?

Score

24. Are emergency personal supplies such as flashlights
    on hand for all employees during an evacuation?

25. Do you have a business continuity plan?

26. Has it been tested?

* * *

10 The Insider's Secrets to Good Crisis Planning

"It's better to have the plan and not need it, than to need the plan and not have it."

–Anonymous

The War Room

Smart companies have learned that a crisis cannot be managed in an ordinary conference room. For companies with extensive operations, the crisis center becomes Mission Control. Look, for example, at FedEx Emergency Central, as described on CNN:

> Supplies are a critical requirement. Don't leave them to chance. FEMA reminds businesses of some of the basics to have on hand:
>
> Battery-powered radios, and a special radio that can receive weather alerts from the National Oceanographic and Atmospheric Administration (NOAA).
>
> Copies of important records such as site maps, building plans, insurance polices, employee contact information, supplier and shipper contact lists, computer backups, law enforcement contacts, and other priority documents in hard copy in a waterproof, fireproof container; with a backup at a continuity site.

Recommended supplies for employees:
–Water—one gallon of water per person for drinking and sanitation
–Food—at least a three-day supply of non-perishable food
–Flashlight and extra batteries
–First-aid kit and three-day supply of prescription or other medications
–Whistle to signal for help
–Dust mask or cotton t-shirt to help filter the air

–Moist towelletes
–Can opener
–Sturdy shoes, extra clothes and blankets
–Cash
(Source: CNN broadcast, October 3, 2005)

Keep Your Contact Information Connected

Even the best plans may fall apart if the system for notifying crisis team members and other key staff at the onset of a crisis fails. Despite automation, updating many notification systems—e.g., phone numbers—remain a manual process, dependent on periodic checks or reminders to let the keeper of the data know of new mobile and home numbers. The solution is simple one: Connect the crisis plan to all the other inputs—e.g., HR records linked to the plan, so that changes click in when they are made.

Consider All Risks

Forget probability tables. If anyone had considered the possibility of two passenger planes being deliberately flown into the World Trade Center, it would have been so low on the probability scale that the right questions would never have been asked. Well, it did happen, and the improbable and impossible may happen again.

It is not impossible to imagine the extreme situations. While you will never define them all, a free-thinking meeting of departments defining the predictable and extreme scenarios will yield a manageable list, to which you should then ask all the "what if" questions—specifically:

–If this happened, would we be prepared to face it?

–What needs to be done to prepare?

–Can we prevent this?

–Are we fostering open communication to prevent a crisis?

The Headquarters Crisis Plan is not Enough

Each location and operation of the company should have its own crisis plan, modeled after the home office crisis plan but tailored to the needs of the location and operation. This is especially important given the increasing number of off-shore operations. In order to facilitate the creation of the localized crisis plans, it is useful to provide each location with a tool kit or template for the creation of their crisis plan.

Crisis Teams—The Who and the How

Organization patterns for crisis teams vary. In many corporations—especially those with high risk or regulated businesses such as transportation or chemicals—the leaders in the crisis function tend to be in the security, or health and safety departments. In other, seemingly less crisis-prone companies, they may be in corporate communications. In reality, the most reasonable answer is a partnership among the three functions—security, health and safety, and communications. In some of the largest corporations, the CEO may never become involved in a crisis unless and until it reaches huge proportions. In others, the CEO is immediately informed and may lead the crisis team.

Well-defined crisis teams are essential elements of a crisis plan. The most effective structure is a simple one, consisting of:

The Senior Crisis Team, chaired by the CEO. In many companies it also is appropriate to create brand-specific crisis teams, headed by the brand CEOs. In both cases, the team members typically include the senior executives for communications, human resources, legal, operations or manufacturing, customer service and sales and marketing.

The Crisis Support Teams, which include a defined number of support staff for each area, charged with carrying out the decisions of the Senior Crisis Team.

Go Teams, comprised of trained volunteers from mid-management ranks who can be sent to the site of a serious incident to offer support and logistical assistance to customers and employees.

Employee Emergency Team, charged with tracking, communicating with and caring for the needs of employees in a serious incident in which employees may have lost their homes, or may be required to work at off-site locations because their work locations may have been adversely affected.

Business Continuity Team, whose function is to plan and implement the company's continuity plan in the aftermath of an incident which may have shut down one or more facilities.

Business Continuity Planning

Business Continuity, once the sleepy function that few cared about, has become an urgent concern, especially since the events of 9/11. In 2004, the SEC approved the NYSE and NASD proposed requirements for listed company's business continuity obligations:

NYSE Rule 446 and NASD Rules 3510 and 3520 outline a set of 10 minimum requirements that must be addressed, regardless of the size of the member company:

Ten Minimum Compliance Elements

(1) Books and records backup and recovery (hard copy and electronic).
(2) Identification of all mission-critical systems and backup for such systems
(3) Financial and operational risk assessments
(4) Alternate communications between customers and the firm
(5) Alternate communications between the firm and its employees
(6) Alternate physical location of employees
(7) Critical business constituent, bank and counter-party activity
(8) Regulatory reporting
(9) Communications with regulators
(10) Method of assuring customers prompt access to their funds and securities in the event the member or member organization determines it is unable to continue its business

There is now a significant amount of professional activity taking place in this specialty, and virtually everything current can be found in the free weekly online newsletter, *Continuity Central*, published in London. Highly recommended! (www.continuitycentral.com)

How quickly your company can get back to business after a terrorist attack or tornado, fire or flood often depends on emergency planning done today. Start planning now to improve the likelihood that your company will survive and recover.

The Department of Homeland Security provides a useful overview of business continuity planning:

- Carefully assess how your company functions, both internally and externally, to determine which staff, materials, procedures and equipment are absolutely necessary to keep the business operating.
- Review your business process flow chart, if one exists.
- Identify operations critical to survival and recovery.
- Include emergency payroll, expedited financial decision-making and accounting systems to track and document costs in the event of a disaster.
- Establish procedures for succession of management. Include at least one person who is not at the company headquarters, if applicable.
- Identify your suppliers, shippers, resources and other businesses you must interact with on a daily basis.
- Develop professional relationships with more than one company to use in case your primary contractor cannot service your needs. A disaster that shuts down a key supplier can be devastating to your business.
- Create a contact list for existing critical business contractors and others you plan to use in an emergency. Keep this list with other important documents on file, in your emergency supply kit and at an off-site location.
- Plan what you will do if your building, plant or store is not accessible. This type of planning is often referred to as a continuity of operations plan, or COOP, and includes all facets of your business.
- Consider if you can run the business from a different location or from your home.
- Develop relationships with other companies to use their facilities in case a disaster makes your location unusable.
- Plan for payroll continuity.
- Decide who should participate in putting together your emergency plan.
- Include workers from all levels—both in planning and as active members of the emergency management team.
- Consider a broad cross-section of people from throughout your organization, but focus on those with expertise vital to daily business functions. These will likely include people with technical skills as well as managers and executives.
- Define crisis management procedures and individual responsibilities in advance.
- Make sure those involved know what they are supposed to do.
- Train others in case you need back-up help.
- Coordinate with others.
- Meet with other businesses in your building or industrial complex.
- Talk with first responders, emergency managers, community organizations and utility providers.

–Plan with your suppliers, shippers and others you regularly do business with.

–Share your plans and encourage other businesses to set in motion their own continuity planning and offer to help others.

–Review your emergency plans annually. Just as your business changes over time, so do your preparedness needs. When you hire new employees or when there are changes in how your company functions, you should update your plans and inform your people.

(Source: United States Department of Homeland Security)

* * *

11   Validating the Crisis and Continuity Plans to Keep Them Alive

E ven the best-looking plan is dead on arrival if it is simply filed away for the day it may be needed. A crisis plan is a living document that should be used for training, simulating and briefing new employees and crisis team members. Anything short of that is ineffective.

Don't forget the small stuff

While an entire book could be devoted to details of crisis preparedness, we mention details here because lack of attention to small details could hamper or shut down a crisis response, or severely hamper it.

Consider some of the small stuff:

—Do enough people have the right phones?

—Do they have spare batteries and power chargers?

—Does everyone have the right ID to give them access to what may become restricted areas?

The Crisis Room

The crisis room, command center or war room, as it is sometimes called, is one of the most important details. The crisis team needs a place to work. It can be a simple conference room used for everyday purposes but immediately available in a crisis. Or it can be elaborate. Airlines have some of the better-developed crisis command centers. At American Airlines, the strategic command center is a vast room featuring a large, horseshoe-shaped table with fully equipped work stations and a conference call line that can accommodate as many as 200 outside callers. Large-screen television monitors set up to receive satellite broadcasts allow command center employees to monitor all news coverage of the crisis. (Source: Paul Argenti, **Harvard Business Review**, December 1 2002)

Minimum Requirements for a Functioning Crisis Room:

–Phone and laptop ports at each seat

–Multidirectional speaker phone

–TV monitors, maps, and white boards on the walls

–Copier, printer, and fax

–Easels with flip chart

And make certain that, in the event of a crisis:

–You have access to cash

–The company can handle a barrage of phone calls from the media, customers and suppliers (assuming the phones are working)

–The company's travel agent has access to charter flight operators if you need to send a team to a crisis site.

Practice Makes Almost Perfect

How to decide on and conduct the training and drills that work—with tips for crisis prevention and continuous improvement?

A number of formats are available for simulations. And some of the best are the simplest and shortest. In each case, a maximum of two staff members should be designated in advance as the "trusted agents" who design the scenario in strict confidence. The most effective scenario is one that:

–Has never occurred at the company

–Is based on one of the known risks the company faces

–Is clearly described and is challenging

–May have occurred at some other company

Tabletop Exercise
Time Commitment: 2 hours
The advantage of this format, which is conducted around a conference table, is that it is informal. The team is given a scenario, and team members are asked to provide their action plans in line with their responsibilities. This is a good refresher for experienced teams, and provides an opportunity to discuss new vulnerabilities.

Simulated Press Conference
Time Commitment: 1 hour
This exercise, best combined with a half-day crisis training session, is based on a scenario posed to the team. Once the team is given the scenario, they are given time to develop a strategy for solutions and key communications messages which would be conveyed during the mock press conference.

During this time they also choose the spokesperson for the group. It may be the senior executive or another, depending on the situation and their judgment of who will be the best and most appropriate person for the job. They are encouraged to rehearse informally before facing the simulated press conference. For the simulation, facilitators, trainers and other staff are generally recruited to play the media and ask the tough questions. The event is recorded on video and then played back for critique. When time permits, a second round is conducted, with either an escalation of the original scenario or a new scenario.

Full Simulation
Time Commitment: 4 hours
This is a full test for the team and any support they may call upon within the organization. Ideally, this should be an unannounced event, testing the immediate response of the senior crisis team and the availability of alternates if needed. The simulation begins with a phone call to the duty officer or crisis team chair, in which an employee, reporter, government official or other source announces a problem that would call for an immediate response. Using a set of "rules of engagement," the team then begins to work together as if the problem were actually occurring. A drill controller is present in the room, periodically giving the team additional details and developments.

An effective simulation also includes a press conference at some point.

During the exercise, the team is allowed to call upon any resources in the company, provided that every call, fax or email is prefaced by, and ends with, the phrase: THIS IS A DRILL. This format is the most effective and ideally should be conducted twice a year.

The Secrets to Media Success

The First Minutes and Hours

If your crisis is already being covered on TV and online, this is the time to join the media. Like it or not, this critical first hour is your chance to establish your credibility. If you do not, CNN and the others will look for "experts" to fill the void and begin commenting and speculating on what has gone wrong. Usually they are wrong. Waiting too long while the others talk about you will create a bigger problem in the long run, as you try and catch up when you can.

Interestingly, you do not need to say very much in this first hour. Great if you can, but you often do not have enough facts. A simple acknowledgement of the crisis: "Such and such has happened at location X. Rescue teams are on the scene. We do not have any details at this time. Our first priority is rescuing the people inside." Simple? It works. It's true. It shows you care and are dealing with the problem. It also shows you're not hiding.

So you are in the midst of a crisis, and your company is besieged with media representatives who want to know what happened, who's been hurt or killed, what damage has been done, and what's being done about it.

These are simple questions with often complex answers that need to be put in context so that the reporter, often lacking expertise in your company or industry, can understand all this and get the story straight.

They Have a Job to Do, and So Do You

Any media briefing or interview is pointless unless you have a point or message.

Experiences in a variety of situations have shown that any audience—your employees, or the general public, for example—will absorb an average of three messages at any one time. And in a crisis, the best messages are ones that show compassion, especially if there have been injuries or deaths; a commitment to solve the crisis; and an explanation of the actions underway.

In crafting these messages, it is very important to give life to them or prove them, with illustrations, simple statistics, or an anecdote. In the best of situations, your messages and their proofs become quotable for the media. Long-winded messages will bore the media and stand little chance of reaching the public. Shorter messages will attract their attention. Think about a message that, with its proof, runs less than a minute.

The difficulty many spokespersons face is making certain they get their messages across. What, you ask, do I do if the reporter never asks the right question that fits my messages?

Answer the questions. But look for the first moment when you can say, "But I would also like to point out…" or "The real issue here is…" and give your most important message. Look for other openings when you can give the others. The reporter will let you do it—after all, you are making news. This technique, called bridging, is simple. The tough part is to remember to do it.

What Can I Do to Overcome Stage Fright?

First, forget that oft-quoted "research" that shows that people would rather die than get up and give a speech or face the media. It is utter nonsense. But stage fright *is* real. It also can be overcome.

Remember:

You know more than the audience.

Most audiences want to hear what you have to say. Yes, some can be hostile—and we will talk about them in a bit. But most are not.

Now for the practical:

The more you know the subject, and the messages or text, the more comfortable you will be.

You need to own the words. The best presentation, talk or interview is the one you own—write it, edit it, make the words yours. The words must ring true to you.

Walking onto a stage carrying words someone else has written for you, and that you've not reviewed and rewritten to create ownership, is a sure path to the jitters. If you have a speech writer, great. It's a huge help for a busy schedule. But it's not a panacea. You still need to edit it, change it, and make it yours.

Read it over and over and over—as many as six times. Make changes as you read. It may be a word here and a word there, or it may be whole paragraphs that need fine-tuning. But take the time to do it. And do it the day before. Not an hour before. That's a sure-fire way to create panic and stage fright.

Then relax before the speech. Take time out. I'm reminded of the time a few years ago when I walked into the office of a CEO I had prepared to face an aggressive press conference. We had spent several hours doing role play, and he was very good, but when I walked into his office an hour before the event, there were a number of executives hovering around his desk, saying things like, "Well, if you don't want to do it, don't do it." I quickly sensed he was getting cold feet, trying to avoid a press event he could not avoid without risking serious embarrassment. I politely asked everyone to leave and closed the door, after which I asked the CEO what his problem was. He replied that even though the preparation had gone well, the reality was daunting for him, since he had never faced an actual aggressive press corps. I told him in no uncertain terms that he was excellent at it, and that he had no choice. I then suggested he go to the company fitness center and go on the treadmill for 45 minutes—which was something he did every day—and then I would meet him and walk with him to the press conference. He did just that and was terrific under pressure.

Some Tried and True, Essential Rules for Working with the Media

–**Nothing is ever off the record.** In today's highly competitive media world, there have been violations of the "off the record" trust. It never was a wise idea to be circumspect, and it is true today. If it is worth saying, it is worth saying on the record. If not, simply do not say it.

–**Avoid saying "No comment."** It is quickly perceived as "I'm hiding something." If you cannot comment, at least explain why you cannot. "This is in litigation and for obvious reasons we cannot comment at this point." There. You've explained why, removing the specter of hiding something.

–**Do not criticize the media when speaking to reporters.** Strong as the temptation may be, it accomplishes nothing to berate the media for unfair coverage, and it could anger many. It is far more productive to strongly set the record straight, working toward more balanced coverage. Some year ago, one of the oil companies, irritated over some stories about the company in *The Wall Street Journal*, made a big announcement that they were cancelling all their advertising in the *Journal* because of what they perceived as biased reporting. It did nothing to change the *Journal*'s writing, but it did create headlines over the cancellation itself.

—**Insist on background information about the reporters you are to face.** While this is not practical for a roomful of reporters you are to face at a press conference, it is practical and useful to know about the reporter you are going to face in a one-on-one interview.

—**Keep eye contact with the reporter.** This conveys trust and credibility. When you shift eye contact, you give the impression you are hiding something or are avoiding the question.

—**Do not repeat negatives.** For example, if you are asked, "Isn't it true that you fear losing market share if the product is recalled?" and you answer, "No, I do not fear loss of market share, etc., etc.," this gives the reporter quotable material to work with. "Joe Jones, president of the XYZ Company, says he 'does not fear loss of market share.'" If your answer is "No, I cannot speculate, but what I can tell you about the actions we have taken," etc, you have gone in a positive direction.

That said, there are no guarantees that the story will please you 100%. But the more control you exercise of what you say and how you say it, the greater the chances of balanced writing in the newsroom.

—**Be yourself.** Do not suddenly take on a new persona for the media. If, for example, you gesture naturally, do so. But if you do not, do not suddenly become a gesturer. It will come across as artificial and distracting.

Understand How to Communicate Risk

Health and safety issues are especially sensitive areas, and you can do more harm than good if you do not follow some of the tested guidelines. Follow the guidelines for communicating with employees and the public, and chances are you can prevent or reduce panic, and offer genuine life-saving information.

—Listen to the concerns of employees and the public. If you do not listen to them, don't expect them to listen to you. Rapid opinion polls, focus groups, blogs, and other sources of feedback should be used.

—Recognize that people will have many uncertainties—on an emotional as well as a practical or logistical level.

–Be honest, frank, and open. They need to trust you and the others you have chosen as spokespersons. Disclose information in plain and complete terms. Do not hide anything. Communicate quickly and often. Do not speculate. And do not reduce the situation to statistics. People do not want to hear that they may have a 1 in 10 chance of dying. They want to know what is being done to help them, and what they can do to help themselves.

–Collaborate with credible experts from universities, government agencies, and health and safety organizations. Two reasons: They can provide useful information, and you can add to your credibility by quoting these recognized and trusted experts. People will respect the expertise you've brought to the table.

–Be honest and open with the media.

–And, above all, speak clearly and with compassion. Express your sympathies up front. People will appreciate it. Use simple, non-technical language. Use examples when appropriate, but avoid comparisons. Different people react differently to comparisons, and some may become outraged at comparisons that seem to trivialize their fears.

Employees Count

When an explosion rocks a building, a terrorist bomb explodes, or a fire breaks out, employees first want to know that their families are safe and that their families know they are safe. Nothing counts more; smart companies will recognize this and provide the means for employees to communicate— as soon as possible, and before asking them to do anything else.

Concern for employees should be at the top of the crisis response list, for without employees a company does not exist. In order for employees to do their jobs, they need to feel safe, and they need to know from senior management that their safety is a top priority.

As we have seen with the experiences of Katrina, the companies which recovered most quickly were those that had plans for finding their employees and providing housing for them.

A number of steps can be put in place to find employees during a crisis:

–On site: Set up an electronic system that notes entries and exits, with the ability to create a log of who is in the building and who is not.

—Off site: Set up a call-in number where any employee—a mile away at a meeting or traveling out of town or overseas—can call and leave an "I'm OK" message.

—Centralize travel arrangements with one agency (or with the company-wide in-house department) so that you can ask for a rapid report on who is traveling and where they are should an emergency hit.

Some Crises Can be Prevented

The best crisis is the one that never happens

Some crises can be prevented, but it takes organization, determination, and listening skills. Organized prevention programs have the potential for the greatest gain at the least cost, but ironically, it is an area most often ignored.

The *Never Say Never* Crisis Prevention Prescription:

Heed early warnings. Katrina and the devastation it caused in the Gulf region are a primary example of warnings ignored. Engineers had warned for years that the region could not withstand a Category 5 hurricane. While the warnings were largely ignored by government agencies, the smart companies in the region planned and practiced for the day.

Take the real crises seriously. One misstep can be excused if you have a strong reserve of good will. Apologize and promise to take steps and then take them. The airline tarmac delays mentioned in Chapter 3 are an example. The airlines know the problem, and at least one airline has pledged passengers will never again wait up to 10 hours on an icy tarmac, headed to nowhere. If the wakeup call for JetBlue shocked them into crisis, their pledge of never again, assuming it is carried out, can prevent the next crisis.

Listen to customers. Customers are the closest you will get to the product. Many companies ask for customer feedback. The ones who benefit from this feedback are the ones who avoid the next problem. The problem with many feedback mechanisms is that some are simply too time-consuming to complete, and others are too superficial to be of any value.

Think of ways to make the feedback process easy for your customers. Keep the forms short but not superficial. In fact, focus groups can help show the flaws in your feedback system and make it better. Do your customers, for example, have no time to provide anonymous feedback on yes-or-no type forms? Would they prefer a personal call? Would they prefer an online mechanism? Do they want a chance to win a reward for taking part? Would they prefer a charitable contribution made by the company for every completed feedback form?

It's no surprise that customers who volunteer comment are those who have had a bad experience. Watch the blogs. They often will reveal problems by those customers who have little or no confidence in the company feedback mechanisms and are taking the criticism into their own hands.

Listen to employees. Employees—especially those on the front lines of operations and customer service—see and hear firsthand the pulse of the company and its customers. Providing easy ways for them to offer suggestion that can prevent problems and crises can pay back in small and big ways. When employees are encouraged to offer ideas for crisis prevention, they will be forthright and enthusiastic. They will appreciate your efforts when they know they are being heard, and when they are rewarded in some tangible way when their ideas are put into practice. Remember that employees need a variety of ways to provide their ideas—these may include a special email suggestion box, a write-in address, and a voice-mail box.

Learn from Experience

Whether you've weathered an actual crisis or gone through the rigors of a simulation, one of the most critical steps to take is the debrief—asking everyone involved for their reactions to the experience and the process that guided them. From this debrief, you will inevitably find that changes can be made so you will be better prepared the next time around. You even may discover some procedures that should be changed in order to prevent a crisis from occurring.

In almost all debriefs, lessons surface, revealing steps that can be taken to prevent a crisis. Some of the ideas are small, some large. These lessons may show, for example, that the public address system does not work in all parts of the building, that a security gate is not staffed properly, or that the business continuity site you thought was perfect cannot be reached easily in a huge crush of traffic.

Every lesson and observation, large or small, when followed through, can help prevent a crisis—or least prevent an emergency from escalating to a crisis. Lives may be saved.

The debrief can take many forms. For example, immediately following a simulation, while the entire team is still in the same room, use the opportunity to go around the table and ask each person to give a 4-5 minute rundown of what, in their view, went well and what needs improvement. If their input requires more detail, they should be charged with writing that up immediately after the meeting.

If a crisis has occurred that involved dozens of resources within the company and with outside agencies such as vendors and government agencies, assign someone to conduct interviews with all parties to determine the lessons learned. This, too, should be done immediately.

Finally, if the crisis has involved a small team of perhaps 6 to 8 staff members, a more expedient method would be to ask each to complete a form on which they are asked a number of questions:

(1) Were you notified promptly?

(2) Were you able to reach all the members of the crisis team promptly?

(3) Did you receive a constant flow of information?

(4) Were you able to coordinate with the crisis site so that you could be helpful?

(5) How promptly and thoroughly were media calls handled?

(6) Was media coverage balanced and accurate?

(7) Was a call center set up to handle calls from customers or employees' families? How effective was that effort?

(8) Were the call center personnel trained and equipped to handle the calls?

Travel in the Post-9/11 Era

Business travel has become more complicated since 9/11, though to see the full-to-capacity flights today, there does not appear to be any cutback. Nonetheless, there are delays and hassles going through security, occasional evacuations of airports when a suspicious package is found, and the ever-changing rules of what can and cannot be taken aboard a plane.

There are no signs that global business travel is about to disappear, so the smart executives will conduct themselves smartly. This includes but is not limited to the following suggestions:

–Use common sense. Don't go to areas after dark that are known to be unsafe.
–Learn to pack lightly—and carry your bags on.
–Be careful on busy streets. Hold on to your belongings and do not stop to answer questions from passersby–the odds are too great they are looking to catch you off guard and steal your wallet or purse.
–Employees traveling to international destinations present a specific challenge, and experienced business travel departments sign up with one of the international emergency services. They provide country-specific travel advisories, briefings on local business protocols and customs, and emergency aid. Two of the most prominent are International SOS and iJet.

Crises Abroad—What the State Department Does and Does Not Do

The Process Earthquakes, hurricanes, political upheavals, acts of terrorism, and hijackings are only some of the events threatening the safety of Americans abroad. Each event is unique and poses its own special difficulties. However, for the State Department there are certain responsibilities and actions that apply in every disaster or crisis.

When a crisis occurs, the State Department's Bureau of Consular Affairs sets up a task force or working group to bring together all the people necessary to work on that event. Usually this Washington task force will be in touch by telephone 24 hours a day with the ambassador and Foreign Service officers at the embassy in the country affected.

In a task force, the immediate job of the Bureau of Consular Affairs is to respond to the thousands of concerned relatives and friends who begin to telephone the State Department immediately after the news of a disaster is broadcast.

Relatives want information on the welfare of their family members and on the disaster. For hard information, the State Department relies on its embassies and consulates abroad. Often these installations are also affected by the disaster and lack electricity, phone lines, gasoline, etc. Nevertheless, Foreign Service officers work hard to get information back to Washington as quickly as possible. This is rarely as quickly as the press is able to relay information. Foreign Service Officers cannot speculate; their information must be accurate. Often this means getting important information from the local government, which may or may not be immediately responsive.

As concerned relatives call in, officers of the Bureau of Consular Affairs collect the names of the Americans possibly involved in the disaster and pass them to the embassy and consulates. Officers at the site attempt to locate these Americans in order to report on their welfare. The officers work with local authorities and, depending on the circumstances, may personally search hotels, airports, hospitals, or even prisons. As they try to get information, their first priority is Americans dead or injured.

Death   When an American dies abroad, the Bureau of Consular Affairs must locate and inform the next of kin. Sometimes this is difficult. If the American's name is known, the Bureau's Office of Passport Services will search for his or her passport application. However, that information may not be current.

The Bureau of Consular Affairs provides guidance to grieving family members on how to make arrangements for local burial or return of the remains to the U.S. The disposition of remains is affected by local laws, customs, and facilities that are often vastly different from those in the U.S. The Bureau of Consular Affairs relays the family's instructions, and necessary private funds to cover the costs involved, to the embassy or consulate. The Department of State has no funds to assist in the return of remains or ashes of American citizens who die abroad. Upon completion of all formalities, the consular officer abroad prepares an official Foreign Service Report of Death, based upon the local death certificate, and sends it to the next-of-kin or legal representative for use in U.S. courts to settle estate matters.

A U.S. consular officer overseas has statutory responsibility for the personal estate of an American who dies abroad if the deceased has no legal representative in the country where the death occurred. The consular officer takes possession of personal effects, such as convertible assets, apparel, jewelry, personal documents and papers. The officer prepares an inventory and then carries out instructions from members of the deceased's family concerning the effects. A final statement of the account is then sent to the next-of-kin. The diplomatic pouch cannot be used to ship personal items, including valuables, but legal documents and correspondence relating to the estate can be transmitted by pouch. In Washington, the Bureau of Consular Affairs gives the next of kin guidance on procedures to follow when preparing letters testamentary, letters of administration, and affidavits of next-of-kin as acceptable evidence of legal claim of an estate.

Injury   When an American is injured abroad, the local embassy or consulate notifies the task force, which notifies family members in the U.S. The Bureau of Consular Affairs can assist in sending private funds to the injured American. Frequently it collects information on the individual's prior medical history and forwards it to the embassy or consulate. When necessary, the State Department assists in arranging the return of the injured American to the U.S. commercially, with appropriate medical escort, via commercial air ambulance or, occasionally, by U.S. Air Force medical evacuation aircraft. The use of Air Force facilities for a medical evacuation is authorized only under certain stringent conditions, and when commercial evacuation is not possible. The full expense must be borne by the injured American or his family.

Evacuation Sometimes commercial transportation entering and leaving a country is disrupted during a political upheaval or natural disaster. If this happens, and if it appears unsafe for Americans to remain, the embassy and consulates will work with the task force in Washington to charter special air flights and ground transportation to help Americans depart. The U.S. Government cannot order Americans to leave a foreign country. It can only advise and try to assist those who wish to leave.

The Privacy Act The provisions of the Privacy Act of 1974 are designed to protect the privacy and rights of Americans, but occasionally they complicate efforts to assist citizens abroad. As a rule, consular officers may not reveal information regarding an individual American's location, welfare, intentions, or problems to anyone, including family members and Congressional representatives, without the expressed consent of that individual. Although they may be sympathetic to the distress this can cause concerned families, consular officers must comply with the provisions of the Privacy Act.

(Source: Bureau of Consular Affairs, U.S. Department of State)

What to Do When the Color-Coded Threat Levels Change

The Department of Homeland Security created the color-coded terrorism threat level system soon after the department was created. The system, intended as a warning to government and business, has drawn criticism because it does not provide advice to businesses on what to do at each level. With specific actions at each level, this can be a useful system.

In practice, some locations or certain industries from time to time are segmented and put on special alerts.

Following are some official and unofficial suggestions:

Green–Low
–Low risk of terrorist attacks

–Maintain crisis plan protocols, including updates, training and preventive procedures.

Blue–Guarded
–General risk of terrorist attacks

Yellow–Elevated
–Review physical security of all locations.
–Review access procedures for all visiting vehicles; consider an inspection procedure for all visiting vehicles.
–Remove trash containers and newspaper vending machines that could be used for bombs or other explosives.
–Monitor the media for possible incidents or additional warnings.

Orange - High
–Increase surveillance of critical locations.
–Take additional precautions at public events.
–Inspect all deliveries, including mail and messenger packages.
–Discontinue tours.
–Verify that all alternate work sites are ready for use if needed.
–Verify that all infrastructure at an alternate site is ready to operate.
–Restrict access to essential or cleared personnel only.

Red–Severe
–Remove all vehicles from property unless owners are clearly identified.
–Look for CEO COM LINK^{SM} calls, if you are registered.

Register for Access to CEO COM LINK^{SM}

The Critical Emergency Operations Communications Link (CEO COM LINK^{SM}) is a secure telephone network that can be activated to discuss a threat or crisis. When CEOs are alerted that the system is being activated, they dial in to a secure conference-call number. Each caller goes through a multi-step authentication process to ensure that only authorized participants are on the CEO COM LINK^{SM} calls.

The calls allow senior government officials to brief CEOs on developments and threats. The calls also allow CEOs to ask questions or share information with government leaders and with each other. Business rules have been established to govern calls and handle sensitive information.

CEO COM LINK^{SM} is activated when there is a need for the federal government and CEOs to exchange information quickly, securely and efficiently during a threat or crisis.

CEO COM LINK^{SM} requires advance registration and training. Each CEO who is part of the system is issued a means of authentication so a caller's identity can be verified. For additional information, contact the Business Roundtable.

Get to know the government before they get to know you

A complex array of documents and procedures has emerged from the Department of Homeland Security since its creation following 9/11. A veritable alphabet soup of procedures would require an entire book to explain the basics. These documents and procedures continue to emerge and will be with us for the foreseeable future. While they are complex and often Byzantine, they should not be ignored. The simple fact is: in an emergency of severe proportions, they will affect the actions and outcomes of private enterprise.

The National Response Plan alone is comprised of five complex elements: the Domestic Readiness Group, coordinated by the White House; the Incident Advisory Council; the National Operations Center; the Strategic Information Operations Center; and the Principal Federal Official.

In the event of a severe emergency:

–You may lose some or all control over your operations.

–You may be called upon to contribute necessary items and services to an impacted area.

Become familiar with some of the central documents—specifically the National Response Plan and the National Incident Management System. They are complex documents that spell out, in theory at least, what might occur during an extreme event.

Get to know your local government resources and what they can and cannot do. In a crisis, details and resources count. For example, if you have operations in suburban or smaller townships and you require a bomb squad to take over a suspicious package, do not assume they have a bomb squad —or if they do, that it can handle more than one call at a time. If you know that in advance of any event, you would be wise to have a commercial bomb squad on tap.

Finally—What can you do to make this all work?

As mentioned earlier, the goal for any company, regardless of size, should be to have a senior executive, or possibly two or three co-equals, reporting to the CEO, responsible for crisis readiness and response. At forward-acting companies and others that are not quite prepared yet, a smart practice would be to create a Crisis Planning Committee. The committee, with senior executives representing key departments on the crisis team, would have oversight for the crisis readiness and response strategy, and in particular responsibility for carrying through the lessons learned from each simulation and actual crisis.

* * *

12 Ideas Beyond the Norm – Or – Why Aren't We Doing That?

Grief or Assistance?

All too often we hear, in the wake of a tragedy, that the company or organization is providing "grief counselors." Grief is a very private emotion, and it is difficult to believe that employees or customers who have been involved in a life-threatening or tragic experience want to meet total strangers who—though qualified—will begin soothing their grief as if they were their own clergymen, analysts, or close friends. What people really need in the wake of these experiences is assistance—with transportation, medical care, and the countless other details they may face. You would be well served to consider, in lieu of or in addition to the "grief counselors," experienced assistance teams that can help smooth the way during a difficult period. Not coincidentally, the better the assistance, the less likelihood of lawsuits and lingering anger.

The Devil's in the Details

In a disaster, when power is lost, cell phones will become indispensable—until they need re-charging. A few devices are now on the market that provide battery charges or boosters for cell phones, another essential part of the emergency supply room.

Don't give up on all the traditional landline phones. Have at least one in the house in case the local cells go down.

And ATM's operate on electricity. So have some cash on hand.

Remind employees to designate a friend or family member outside the crisis area as a central contact, so that others in the family can contact that one person for news.

Broaden the Scope of Crisis Training

Israel's Egged Bus Company prepares for contingencies by training key employees to be able to take over another completely different job if needed in an emergency. The concept, called multiskilled training, Egged reports, has other benefits, creating new friendships, a stronger sense of their individual value, and greater appreciation of the big picture.

An Expiration Date

We all know that crisis plans need to be kept up to date. A stale plan is useless. One way to remind all that the plan needs to be updated is to post a prominent expiration date on the plan. Imagine picking up a plan with an expired date when a crisis hits. It will not occur twice.

An Invitation to Government

Add a new dimension to your simulations by inviting local government representatives to observe them. Emergency management authorities from police to fire to the mayor's office can gain a greater understanding of your business and crisis plans, and add valuable perspective during the debrief.

Won't a Video Solve all the Problems?

A common question:

"I have no time for crisis drills," say some CEOs, "no matter how much you try to convince me. So I made a great video telling everyone in the company how important it to be crisis-ready. Isn't that enough?"

No. A video, no matter how well produced it is and how compelling you are, is window dressing. It may make you feel as though you've done something, but you really haven't. Five minutes after the mandatory screening for all employees, everyone goes back to work and forgets it. What really counts is a commitment and program where plans are created and tested.

Looking for a Fresh Approach to Risk Assessment?

Go beyond the basics and ask some tough questions: If you were an ex-employee with complete freedom to say what you wanted to say, what risks would you list? And if you were an investigative journalist turned loose in inside the company, what risks would you find?

Emergency Supplies

–When preparing for emergency situations, it's best to think first about the basics of survival: fresh water, food, clean air, and warmth. Encourage everyone to have a portable kit customized to meet their personal needs, with essential medications and two battery-powered radios. A commercial radio is a good source for news and information from local authorities. An NOAA weather radio can alert you to weather emergencies or announcements from the Department of Homeland Security. Get one with tone-alert feature, if possible, which automatically alerts you when a watch or warning is issued in your area. (Tone-alert is not available in some areas.) Include extra batteries.

–Keep copies of important records such as site maps, building plans, insurance policies, employee contact and identification information, bank account records, supplier and shipping contact lists, computer backups, emergency or law enforcement contact information and other priority documents in a waterproof, fireproof portable container. Store a duplicate set at an off-site location.

–Talk to your co-workers about what emergency supplies the company can feasibly provide, if any, and which ones individuals should consider keeping on hand.

Recommended emergency supplies include the following:
–One gallon of water per person per day, for drinking and sanitation
–Food, at least a three-day supply of non-perishable food
–Battery-powered radio and extra batteries
–Flashlight and extra batteries
–First aid kits
–Whistles to signal for help
–Dust or filter masks, readily available in hardware stores, which are rated based on how small a particle they filter out
–Moist towelettes for sanitation
–Wrenches or pliers to turn off utilities
–Can openers for food (if kit contains canned food)

–Plastic sheeting and duct tape to seal rooms
–Garbage bags and plastic ties for personal sanitation

Budgeting for Preparedness

Ready.gov, the Department of Homeland Security's business preparedness guide, has constructed an interesting budget worksheet on preparedness.

No Cost

–Meet with your insurance provider to review current coverage.
–Create procedures to quickly evacuate and also to shelter-in-place. Practice the plans.
–Talk to your people about the company's disaster plans. Two-way communication is central before, during and after a disaster.
–Create an emergency contact list, including employee emergency contact information
–Create a list of critical business contractors and others whom you will need in an emergency.
–Know what kinds of emergencies might affect your company both internally and externally.
–Decide in advance what you will do if your building is unusable.
–Create a list of inventory and equipment—including computer hardware, software and peripherals—for insurance purposes.
–Talk to utility service providers about potential alternatives, and identify back-up options.
–Promote family and individual preparedness among your co-workers.
–Include emergency preparedness information during staff meetings, in newsletters, on the company intranet, in periodic employee emails, and via other internal communications methods.

Under $500

–Buy a fire extinguisher and smoke alarm.
–Set up a telephone call tree, a password-protected page on the company Website, an email alert, or a call-in voice recording to communicate with employees curing an emergency.
–Provide first aid and CPR training to key employees.
–Use and keep up-to-date anti-virus software and firewalls.
–Attach equipment and cabinets to walls or to other, stable equipment.
–Place heavy or breakable objects on low shelves.

Index

A

B

For sales, editorial information, subsidiary rights information
or a catalog, please write or phone or e-mail
Brick Tower Press
1230 Park Avenue
New York, NY 10128, US
Sales: 1-800-68-BRICK
Tel: 212-427-7139 Fax: 212-860-8852
www.BrickTowerPress.com
email: bricktower@aol.com.

For sales in the United States, please contact
National Book Network
nbnbooks.com
Orders: 800-462-6420
Fax: 800-338-4550
custserv@nbnbooks.com

For sales in the UK and Europe please contact our distributor,
Gazelle Book Services
Falcon House, Queens Square
Lancaster, LA1 1RN, UK
Tel: (01524) 68765 Fax: (01524) 63232
email: gazelle4go@aol.com.

For Australian and New Zealand sales please contact
Bookwise International
174 Cormack Road, Wingfield, 5013, South Australia
Tel: 61 (0) 419 340056 Fax: 61 (0)8 8268 1010
email: karen.emmerson@bookwise.com.au